R. D. Bartlett and Patricia P. Bartlett

Monitors and Tegus

Everything About Selection, Care,
Nutrition, Diseases, Breeding, and Behavior

Filled with Full-color Photographs
Illustrations by Laura Barghusen

BARRON'S

CONTENTS

Understanding Your Monitor or Tegu 5

Choosing a Monitor or Tegu 6

Captive Raised versus Wild Collected 7

Caging 9

Cage Size 9

Cage Furniture 11

Cage/Terrarium Cleanliness 12

Lighting and Heating 13

HOW-TO: Make a Quasi-Natural Outdoor Cage 16

Feeding and Watering Techniques 19

The Menu 19

Feeding 20

Insects: Catching Your Own 21

Insects: Purchasing or Raising 22

Mice and Rats: To Purchase or Breed 25

Vitamin/Mineral Supplements 25

Watering and Hydration Techniques 26

Handling 31

Body Language 32

HOW-TO: Handle Your Monitor or Tegu 36

Health 39

Diet-Related Health Problems 39

Mechanical Injury 42

Pathogens and Parasites 47

Respiratory Disorders 48

Breeding 51

Health 52

Sexing 53

Let's Talk Temperature 55

Introduction to the Monitors 59

The Lizard Family Varanidae 59

Some Pet Store Favorites 63

African Monitors 63

Asian/Indonesian Monitors 69

Australian Monitors 82

A Few Eagerly Sought, but Hard-to-Acquire Monitors 89

Introduction to the Teiids 97

Tegus 98

Amazon Tegus 99

Red and Argentine Tegus 101

Glossary 106

Information 108

Index 110

UNDERSTANDING YOUR MONITOR OR TEGU

The long-bodied, agile monitors and tegus, respectively Old World and New World lizards, display a great deal of morphological variety. For many hobbyists, however, smaller is better when it comes to selecting a pet.

Monitors and Tegus can range in size from 8 inches (20 cm) to 10 feet (3 m), and in temperament from placid to openly hostile. These denizens of deserts, forests, and savannas are active hunters and scavengers, and their caging and feeding must reflect their specialized needs.

The young of a great many monitors—even some that are predominantly terrestrial when adult—are highly arboreal, which keeps many juveniles out of the casual reach of predatory larger specimens. When planning caging, this propensity of the young to climb needs to be considered.

Even the adults of many large monitor species (*large* means adult total length of

Like other water monitors, the white-headed water monitor is a heavy-bodied species that may exceed five feet in length.

4 feet [1.3 m] or more) are agile climbers, readily taking to a tree or other vertical rise to pursue prey or escape danger. Teiids are not quite the climbers that the younger monitors are but, if warm, they are still fast-moving lizards that can dart through a cage opening faster than the keeper can react.

The degree of tameness that you can expect from your monitor or tegu will depend on the species, as well as the amount of gentle handling to which the lizard is subjected. Some species seem better able than others to adjust to the rigors of captive life. The sharp teeth and claws and, to a lesser degree, the whipping tail of a monitor or tegu of even moderate size can discourage friendly overtures by all but the most dedicated keepers. To augment these defensive tactics, frightened monitors will also void their intestinal contents on a careless handler, in itself a discouraging habit.

A portrait of an Amazonian tegu.

Choosing a Monitor or Tegu

Caring for one or more monitor or tegu lizards is an ongoing task, and choosing the wrong species, for whatever reason, can greatly reduce the enjoyment you hoped to feel when you chose your scaly pet.

Unless you are able and willing to provide a nearly room-sized cage for your monitor, you really don't want a Nile or Asian water monitor, and you may not really want a savanna monitor, which is only slightly smaller and has just slightly smaller caging needs.

Even if you are willing to devote a room-sized cage to a Nile monitor, will you be able to provide and keep clean the bathtub-sized water receptacle that these semiaquatic saurians should have?

It is not always easy to find another home for big monitors. This is true even if they're tame, and especially true if they are a little less than wholly trustworthy. Cost, besides space and ready availability, is a factor to most hobbyists.

Along with adult size, health should, of course, be a major deciding factor in the acquisition of any monitor or tegu. The animal you choose should look alert. The eyes should be clear, bright, inquisitive, and rounded, not encrusted, dull, or sunken. The long tongue should be protruded and flicked as the lizard investigates its quarters or a disturbance.

The body weight should be average to heavy, not thin with obviously protruding ribs and pelvis. The skin should not be hanging in loose folds. Whenever possible, watch the animal feed. If kept properly, a healthy monitor that is acclimating well should willingly feed within a day or two after it has been received. If you do not see it feed, we suggest that you not buy it.

Highly aggressive monitors or tegus or those that are otherwise severely stressed should also

The blue tegu is now available in normal (pictured), albino, and snow morphs.

HELPFUL HINT: Wild-collected adult monitors and tegus are poor candidates for a satisfying lizard-owner relationship. Avoid these if you are interested in having an easily handled pet.

An adult of the black and gold morph of the Amazonian tegu.

be avoided. These will often not acclimate to a point where they can be handled and may even refuse to feed in captivity.

Although baby and subadult monitors and tegus can be housed communally, adults tend to live a solitary existence. Males stake out their territories and defend them vigorously against incursions by other males of their species. Females are usually much less territorial.

Two maturing male monitors or tegus that have been housed together since babyhood are very likely to become incompatible with age. Be prepared to provide separate housing when agonistic behavior starts.

Captive Raised versus Wild Collected

Many monitors and tegus are now captive bred by hobbyists in the United States and Europe. Others, most notably the savanna monitor, are farmed in Africa. And still others are collected from the wild. European hobbyists were probably the first to develop an accurate methods of sexing and breeding many monitor species. Tegus are not yet as popular as pet animals, and fewer of them are captive bred. Spiny-tailed monitors, Storr's monitors, mourning monitors, and a few others are now bred with some regularity. A few endangered species, Bengal and desert monitors among them, are captive bred, but because they are expensive lizards and it is necessary to apply for and be issued permits to ship them in interstate

commerce, they are still not commonly seen. Even the magnificent Komodo monitor has now been captive bred. It is probable that the coveted lizard will be available in the pet trade within a few years.

Although many of the more expensive species are captive bred, other popular pet species such as Nile and savanna monitors are so inexpensive in their native Africa that breeders simply could not compete in price. Therefore, no serious captive-breeding programs are yet in place for these pet store species.

We strongly recommend that enthusiasts purchase captive-bred and captive-hatched monitors and tegus when possible.

This ultimately will not only reduce collecting pressures, but also assure you of acquiring acclimated, nonstressed, nearly (or entirely) parasite-free specimens. Although the cost of captive-bred specimens may be slightly greater than that of imported specimens, the difference will be money well spent. In today's increasingly conservation-oriented society, purchasing captive-bred and captive-hatched specimens is the responsible thing to do.

CAGING

A hobbyist's purchase of a monitor, especially of a large species, is all too often wrongly on impulse. Be sure to match your caging and monitor/tegu selection to your available time, space, and money.

When looking at an 8-inch (20-cm) hatchling Savanna monitor or a 10-inch (25-cm) baby Nile monitor, it is hard for a hobbyists, especially a new hobbyist, to visualize the lizard's adult size. If well cared for, that lizard that now fits so comfortably in the 10-gallon (38-L) tank in the pet store will need a 100-gallon or larger enclosure when it is adult. An increase of a hundred times (or more!) in overall bulk is not only possible, but probable. Coupled with the increase in size is the real possibility that the disposition of your adult monitor may not be entirely benign.

It stands to reason that the smaller species of monitors and tegus are easier to house at all stages of their lives than large species. Equally obvious is the fact that if you choose a medium-to-large monitor species, arid-land

Long and motile describes the tongue of this Asian water monitor.

and savanna dwellers are more easily housed than persistently aquatic species. You simply don't need to provide and continually clean a large volume of water (read "swimming pool") for the arid-land forms (see also pages 59 to 101 and individual species accounts).

Cage Size

A monitor of 6 feet (2 m) or more in length should be provided with an enclosure at least the size of a room, furnished with tree trunks and inclined limbs, elevated shelves, access to natural sunlight or a bank of UV (ultraviolet) lights, a hot-spot basking area, areas of seclusion, and an adequate supply of clean water. Indeed, many keepers of large monitors actually donate a spare room to their charge.

No matter the size of the lizards, monitors and tegus that you hope to breed should be provided with proportionately more room than

V. salvadorii, *the crocodile monitor, may exceed the Komodo dragon in length but cannot contend with it in body bulk.*

otherwise, and of course the cages for groups of lizards should be larger yet than for only a single specimen.

Indoor cages can be custom made or adapted from suitably sized aquaria. No matter which, cages must close tightly and lock. Sides must be of welded wire rather than screen, which can be torn by the sharp claws of only moderately large monitors and tegus.

If you choose to make your own wood-framed cage, it is a small matter to hinge and

HELPFUL HINT: Don't let the term *custom made* scare you. Anyone with even moderate carpentry skills can make a suitable cage in an evening. If you know how to hammer, staple, and use a saw, you can make a cage.

secure a top. If the top is separate from the cage, use clamps or place a brick atop each end to discourage unauthorized "wanderings." The precaution may not be attractive, but it is functional.

As your lizard grows, it will require correspondingly more space. Eventually, a large custom-built cage (which will quickly become the focal point of a room)—or the room itself—will be required to house the lizard.

A simple cage begins with a wooden framework. Welded wire mesh is stapled to the outside of the framework. The bottom can be a piece of waterproof plywood (¾ inch [.9 cm] is best, but ½ inch [1.3 cm] will do). The bottom can be wire mesh if the cage sits atop a bed of newspaper. During the colder months, to facilitate warming the cage, you may have to staple

Savanna monitors are stocky and stubby in build.

Pliofilm to the outside; a minimum of 4 mil thickness is suggested. The supporting braces will need to be at least 2 × 2s (5 × 5 cm) or better, 2 × 4s (5 × 10 cm), and the wire mesh 2 × ½ inch (5 × 1.3 cm). A smaller mesh is apt to catch the monitors' and tegus' toenails and could cause injury to the toes. If a smooth welded mesh is used, it will help prevent the lizard from abrading its nose if it tries to escape. The braces can be nailed or screwed together and the mesh stapled on with a staple gun. Be sure the door is large enough for you to reach to the bottom of the cage to clean it, or add another door at the bottom of the cage for this purpose.

If you prefer a heavier cage, you can build one from plywood sheeting with wood-framed glass doors. The plywood cage will require sizable screened ventilation panels on each end. If wire is used in the ventilation panels, make certain it is welded and a large enough mesh to avoid injury.

For moderate to large (2.5 to 4 feet [.8–1.2 m] plus) arboreal monitors, we provide a vertically oriented cage, 6 feet (2 m) in length, and just narrow and low enough to be moved through a doorway—approximately 30 inches (75 cm) wide × 6 feet (2 m) high. This allows the cage to be moved outside in good weather and brought inside in bad weather (and removed from the house in case of emergency).

To facilitate this move, the cage is set on a series of casters (wheels). If your cage is glass, set it on a plywood platform that is on casters. The bigger the casters, the better.

If your monitor or tegu is out of its cage roaming about your room or home much of the time, a somewhat smaller cage would be acceptable. In all cases, your lizard should be able to stretch out its full length to bask.

Cage Furniture

In nature, monitors and tegus often have a home burrow, or crevice, or hollow trunk to which they regularly return after foraging and at night. They are more secure in captivity when such provision is made. Although a custom box can be provided, even a simple closed

HELPFUL HINT: No matter what your caging arrangements are, have a plan in place on what to do if you have to leave home in a hurry. Emergencies do happen and your pets should not pay the price for your lack of planning.

cardboard box with an entrance hole provides security for your lizard. We actually prefer two hiding boxes, one warm and one cooler.

In our outside cages we provide either hollowed limbs or, in quasi-natural cages, rock piles (small species) and/or a labyrinth of buried pipes that double in the winter as hibernacula.

The floor covering of your indoor cage can consist of any number of items. Newspaper,

brown kraft paper, Astroturf, indoor/outdoor carpeting, shredded cypress, aspen shavings, or even rabbit food (compressed alfalfa pellets) are all ideal. Avoid any form of cedar, because the phenols can be toxic to your lizard. In a room-sized cage (or the room itself), vinyl flooring provides an easy-to-clean substrate. The papers, shavings, and rabbit food can be discarded when soiled; the carpets can be washed, dried, and replaced, and the flooring can be mopped. Monitors and tegus may repeatedly defecate in a particular area of their cage. Some specimens defecate in their water dishes, but others will quickly adopt a kitty pan containing a little sand.

Small but sturdy living trees make attractive additions to monitor and tegu cages. The various fig trees (Ficus sp.) and dragon trees (Dracaena sp.) are hardy and tolerant of suboptimal growing conditions.

Plastic plants are a viable alternative. They can be washed as they become soiled. They are generally sturdy enough to bear up under considerable abuse, and you can simply staple the foliage where you want it.

Cage/Terrarium Cleanliness

In the wild, these lizards can move around, so the buildup of organic debris simply does not occur. To maintain suitable cleanliness in captive conditions, you'll probably need to clean your monitor/tegu cage at least twice a week. Water may need even more frequent cleaning. Because carnivorous lizards produce smelly stools, the prompt cleaning is for your sake as much as the lizard's. It is important that you

An outdoor/indoor cage on casters.

A young adult red tegu.

choose the substrate or floor covering that is both safest for the lizard and most easily cleaned and sterilized.

Concerns about salmonella, a common genus of bacteria that can cause gastrointestinal inflammation or infection in humans, mean that you need to keep the cage—and your hands—clean and dispose of all wastes so that they do not contaminate food-preparation or eating areas.

Lighting and Heating

Depending on the species, monitors, tegus, and their relatives have varied lifestyles. They may be arboreal and heliothermic, terrestrial and heliothermic, or semiaquatic and heliothermic.

Note that all three descriptions include the term *heliothermic. Heliothermic* relates to the sun and the temperature.

At optimum, the lizards are most efficient in movement and digestion. Whether kept indoors or out, your monitors and tegus will require adequate heat and light. You will need to duplicate a sunlit habitat within their cage or room. Monitors and tegus like to sprawl while basking. Arboreal species will position themselves lengthwise along a sturdy limb, drooping their legs and part of their tails over the sides. In the wild such basking stations are often above waterways into which the lizards may

drop if startled. Rock-dwelling species often bask in the sunlight in front of a deep fissure or crevice into which they may retreat if disturbed. Terrestrial arid-land dwellers are often encountered in or near concealing patches of shrubby vegetation.

Although you won't be able to provide the waterway, cliff-face exfoliations, or desert shrubs for your lizards, you can provide the light and warm limb or a sandy area on which to sprawl. A limb with bark will be much easier for your lizard to climb and cling to than one that has been peeled.

An elevated basking branch that is of at least the diameter of your lizard's body will be readily used by most species. If the limb is elevated only slightly above floor level, even normally

HELPFUL HINT: Monitors and tegus regulate their body temperatures by basking (thermoregulating) in the sunlight until they attain their optimum body temperature.

An outdoor cage.

terrestrial species may use it extensively. If more than one lizard is present, more than one basking platform should be provided—each illuminated and warmed. The limbs must be securely affixed to prevent toppling.

From above, direct the warming beams of one or two floodlight bulbs onto this perch. A temperature of 95–105°F (35–40.5°C) (measured on the top of the basking limb) should be created. Be certain to position the bulbs so your lizard cannot burn itself if it approaches the lamp. Full-spectrum UVA and UVB incandescent bulbs that *really are* full spectrum are now available. They look like large floodlight bulbs and fit into round metal reflectors. One type is marketed as UVHeat. These bulbs also emit a lot of heat and can be used to warm your lizard's basking area. Do not confuse these with the smaller, less expensive "color-corrected" bulbs that do not provide the same UVA/UVB benefit.

HELPFUL HINT: Light and warmth are mandatory for the long-term well-being of your heliothermic lizards.

It is at a body temperature of 88–95°F (31–35°C) that many heliotherms are most active and disease resistant. Certain desert-dwelling heliothermic lizards may optimally attain even higher body temperatures.

Is full-spectrum (UV-emitting) lighting actually necessary to the well-being of your monitor or tegu? Well, perhaps not absolutely necessary, but the UVA and UVB emissions are beneficial, even when in only small amounts.

UVA helps promote natural behavior in reptiles (see cautions in handling, page 31) and UVB controls the biosynthesis of vitamin D3 in the reptile's skin. When natural biosynthesis occurs, your lizard's dependence on vitamin and mineral supplementation will be lessened somewhat.

Let's look at this in a little more detail.

Truthfully, when it comes to assessing the benefits of artificial UV emissions, the jury is still out. Many keepers of heliothermic lizards consider the use of full-spectrum lighting mandatory. Others, however, have kept and bred these various lizard species without ever using full-spectrum lighting.

We began providing full-spectrum lighting when it was first available, first with Vita-lite, and then more recently with a UVA/UVB incandescent bulb. Lizards provided with full-spectrum lighting, especially UVA, do seem to display more normal behavior than those not so provided. Because normalcy of specimens is what most of us involved in herpetoculture are striving for, we always suggest that UVA/UVB lighting be used. Whatever type of UV light you choose to use, read the label, obey any warning advice and position the light fixture so that

The "black dragon" is an undescribed relative of the water monitor from Malaya.

your lizards can get close enough to the bulb to benefit from it.

Although the new bulbs provide both UVA and UVB lighting, there's another way to provide the same benefits, and it's as close as your back door.

Natural Sunlight

Natural unfiltered sunlight unquestionably provides the best possible lighting (and heat) for any heliothermic lizard. We earlier stressed that your cages be on casters and sized to pass through your doorways. This will enable you to move your lizards—still securely caged—outdoors on warm, sunny days. In most cases the casters will allow a single person to accomplish this otherwise unwieldy task. There is simply nothing better that you can do for your lizards.

Only cages constructed of wood and wire should be placed out in the sun. A glass terrarium not only filters out the UV rays, but, even with a screen top, will intensify and hold heat. This can literally cook your lizards in just a few minutes, even on a relatively cool day! Be sure to provide a shaded area for your lizard even in the wood/wire cages.

If you live in an area where it is absolutely impossible to get your lizard outside, perhaps you could allow it to bask in an opened window on hot summer days. Natural unfiltered sunlight from any vantage point will be of benefit.

More Heating Hints

It can be difficult on a cold northern winter day to provide adequate heat for your monitor

or tegu—especially if it is a very large specimen in a proportionately large cage or if it is loose in its room.

Such devices as thermostatically controlled "hog blankets" (actually a livestock heating pad) can be purchased from many feed stores. Hot rocks can help, but keep a close eye on them to be sure they do not accidentally overheat and burn the lizard. Human heating pads, set on low, or ceramic space heaters will also help either heat the lizard directly or heat its cage or room. No matter which implements you use, be certain that they are thermostatically regulated to a suitable temperature, or that they are enclosed to prevent the lizard from coming in direct contact with them. Many severe reptile burns have occurred on particularly cold days when Herculean efforts are being made to provide sufficient heat. Don't let your lizard become a statistic!

In southwest Florida we were very successful in breeding several species of small monitors in outside, quasi-natural facilities.

The cages were circular, of 8- to 10-foot (2.5–3.2-m) diameter, simple, and relatively inexpensive.

The walls were made from a strip of 3-foot (1-m) aluminum sheeting sunk 1 foot (.3 m) into the ground. We found that the easiest way to

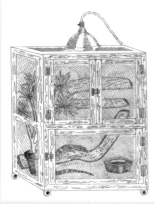

Wood-frame wire cage with hasp on the door, and a door near the bottom to facilitate cleaning.

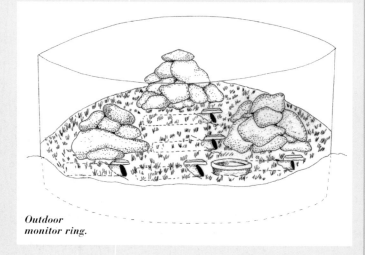

Outdoor monitor ring.

Caging accessories with tegu hiding under plastic plants.

outline and sink the sheeting was to use a posthole digger attached to a 4.5-foot (1.3-m) length of twine. The other end of the twine was noosed loosely around a post tapped into the ground where the center of the cage was to be. By keeping the posthole digger at the outer limit of the twine, it was a relatively simple matter to dig the foot-deep (.3-m) trench needed for the aluminum. No footer was needed. The aluminum sheeting was then set into the trench and leveled (this can be painstaking), and the two ends riveted together. The trench was then filled on both sides, with particular care given to the inside perimeter. Once the

NATURAL OUTDOOR CAGE

filling of the trench was complete, the cage was essentially done. Terra-cotta drain pipes, about 6 inches (15 cm) in diameter, were buried at 45-degree angles for refuges, pyramids of stones were placed strategically, water was supplied, and the lizards were introduced. In our area (Lee County, Florida) these cages worked well, and because predators were not common, required no tops. Where either or both winged and four-footed predators (hawks, crows, cats, raccoons, opossums) are common, a top must be made for these open-air cages. The top can be framed from 1 × 2s (2.5 × 5 m) and covered with ¼-inch (.6-cm) mesh hardware cloth.

With some adaptations, these open topped outdoor cages can be used in many areas of the country. They are, of course, best suited where temperatures are moderate, but with the prudent use of shade cloth (very hot desert areas) or heat tapes (normally cooler regions) many of the smaller monitors and the tegus from more temperate areas can be housed for at least half of the year.

The shade cloth protectors can be held a few feet above the top of the cage on 2 × 4 supports standing on end. If buried a foot and a half in the ground, an 8 foot long 2 × 4 will hold the shade cloth 6½ feet high—high enough for most folks to easily care for the cage the cloth is shielding.

Room-sized caging for monitor.

Keeping the cage suitably warm in naturally cooler areas will require the prudent use of waterproof electrical heating tapes. We have found that the type that are used for preventing outside water pipes from freezing may be rather easily adapted to maintaining warmth in your monitor's or tegu's underground refuge.

An electrician should install the outside junction boxes and all electrical connections used should be certified safe for outdoor usage.

These heating adaptations will only suffice during the summer when all but the low nighttime temperatures are suitable for your lizard's natural activity regimen.

FEEDING AND WATERING TECHNIQUES

Monitors and tegus need variety in their diet to ensure adequate nutrition.

The Menu

Although the larger examples of many of these lizards probably eat a considerable proportion of endothermic (warm-blooded) prey, few (if any) feed exclusively on such items. Rather, most monitors and tegus are actually opportunistic feeders, eagerly accepting a wide variety of food items. Some species preferentially consume mollusks and crustaceans, and at least one monitor and most tegu species include a good amount of fruit in their diet.

Small species consume insects, other arthropods, smaller lizards, and, perhaps, the occasional nestling endotherm (warm-blooded animal). Food items may be alive or in an advanced state of decomposition. Larger species also consume insects, mollusks, crustaceans, and the eggs of birds and reptiles,

African white-throated monitors are large and heavy bodied.

but probably eat a greater overall percentage of vertebrate matter than their smaller relatives. Riverine and estuarine species may incorporate into their diet a great percentage of fish, baby crocodilians, turtles and their eggs, and other aquatic life. Carrion is also accepted.

The largest species of monitors (possibly excepting the slender, arboreal crocodile monitor of Irian Jaya) are formidable predators that are able to chase down and overpower small mammals and virtually anything else they happen across. As with the other groups, carrion also figures prominently in the diet of these largest of lizards (and is one reason why a bite from one of them is immediately infected, should the prey escape being eaten). In contrast, despite its size, the slender crocodile monitor probably feeds extensively on insects and nestling birds.

Diet caution: Although most monitors and tegus, including the highly insectivorous

Varanus olivaceous, Gray's monitor of the Philippines, is one of the few herbivorous monitor species.

Caiman lizards: Less is known about the true dietary needs of the caiman lizards. Once thought to feed exclusively on gastropod and bivalve mollusks, these large, partially aquatic lizards have also been observed eating insects. Captives have eaten fish and canned cat foods.

Feeding

When you hear the crunch of bones as a large monitor or tegu grasps its prey, you know immediately that you need to avoid being bitten by this creature.

The jaws of monitors and tegus are strong, and the teeth are either sharp (occasionally serrate) for cutting or molariform for crushing.

Keepers often enjoy feeding their tegus and monitors by hand, citing their animals as "tame" and "trustworthy." This is an almost sure way to eventually sustain a severe bite. After handling the prey, your hands will smell and taste like the prey. Because monitors determine what's good to eat (most things) or what's not (almost nothing) by scent, taste, and sight, a hand that smells like a mouse or rat will probably be considered a mouse or rat. Do not take the risk. Either place the food in a feeding dish or offer it on very long, blunt-tipped tongs.

Feeding hatchlings: Hatchling and baby monitors kept at optimally warm temperatures can eat from one to several fuzzy mice every second day. Crickets, mealworms, grasshoppers, roaches, and canned foods can also be offered and will usually be accepted. Prekilled food animals should be offered whenever possible.

species, may adapt to a diet of pinky mice, today's reptilian veterinarians question the wisdom of such an obviously artificial diet. It seems that veterinarians are diagnosing a higher percentage of liver problems in lizards fed on an almost exclusive diet of pinky mice. A diet exclusively of crickets has also been allied with liver disorders.

The Philippine Gray's monitor is the only monitor known to incorporate a high percentage of vegetable matter in its diet. Figs and other fruits are eagerly accepted.

Tegus: In general, tegus eat much the same foods as monitors. The big difference is in the amount of vegetation tegus incorporate into their diet. As with captive monitors, a variety of food items is always the best choice.

HELPFUL HINT: A varied diet is best for all lizards. Crickets, grasshoppers, beetles, cockroaches, suitably sized mice, fish, crabs, crayfish, and prepared foods (Zoo-Med and Hill's A/D are manufacturers) should all be offered.

Insects and small mammals are eaten by savanna monitors.

Midsized monitors, (one-fourth to one-half grown) may be fed twice weekly, offering one to several small to medium prekilled mice at each feeding. Continue to offer insects and canned food. Some monitors will eagerly accept prekilled hatchling chicks.

Adult monitors may be fed from one to several large prekilled mice or suitably sized rats twice weekly. Prekilled chicks, large insects, and canned food should also be offered.

Tegus should be offered fare similar to food for like-sized monitors, plus an assortment of fruit.

Feeding prekilled rodents and chicks is not only humane, but will preclude the possibility of the lizard's being injured by its prey.

Force-feeding: It may occasionally be necessary to force-feed ill or severely debilitated monitors and tegus. The force-fed item should be small and easily digested. Canned dog food, cat food, or monitor food moistened with Gatorade may be fed by stomach tube; be certain that you do not put the tube down the windpipe. Gatorade-moistened pinky mice with the body cavity punctured may be gently forced down the lizard's throat. Overfeeding a debilitated lizard will surely cause regurgitation. A small meal, once every two days at first, then

once a day as the lizard's condition improves, will be sufficient. Meal size can be slowly increased as the lizard regains its health. Temperature, stress-free housing, and illumination should be retained at around-the-clock optimum during sickness.

Insects: Catching Your Own

Netting insects from insecticide-free areas is not only a viable option during the warmer months of the year, but also provides your lizard with a supply of the healthiest insects possible. To retain their food value, the insects must be eaten by the lizards within an hour or two after being collected. The type of insects you gather will vary according to the habitat through which you net. Netting through open fields should provide you with a series of grasshoppers, locusts, crickets, and a few other varieties. When netting through shrubby areas, you will usually find a preponderance of caterpillars, leafhoppers, and similar insects. Most of these will be fine for your lizards, and lizards

---

HELPFUL HINT: The amount of food offered should be based on how active your lizard is. The amount should also be varied as necessary, offering more if the lizard looks thin and less if chronic obesity is a problem.

will usually reject those that are noxious after one quick bite.

Insects can also be collected around a porch and beneath streetlights at night. This method of collecting is often more tedious, but on "good" nights may be immensely productive. June beetles and other scarabs and moths are the forms most commonly collected during these nocturnal forays. Big diving beetles and bugs may be encountered in some numbers. These creatures have piercing mouthparts that can injure both you and the lizards. We do not collect these species.

Insects: Purchasing or Raising

It is important that you feed your varanids and teiids only the most nutritious food insects. Unless an insect is continually fed a nutritious diet (gut-loaded), it will provide little food value for your lizards. Maintaining your insects in top-notch health should be a main concern of any herpetoculturist.

The term *gut-loading* refers to feeding your insects an abundance of highly nutritious foods

> **HELPFUL HINT:** A commercially prepared gut-loading diet is now available in the pet marketplace.

immediately before they are offered as food to your lizards. Potatoes alone won't do the job. Calcium, vitamin D3, fresh fruit and vegetables, fresh alfalfa and/or bean sprouts, honey, and vitamin/mineral-enhanced (chick) laying mash are only a few of the foods that may be considered for gut-loading insects.

Many types of insects normally fed to your monitors, tegus, and relatives are commercially available. Your may prefer to buy these commercially available insects. Certainly this is less time consuming than breeding your own insects, and they are available year-round. If you breed your own insects you can ensure that the highest-quality diet is continually fed to them. Even if procuring the insects commercially you should feed them the best diet possible.

Crickets: The gray cricket (*Acheta domesticus*) is bred commercially for fish bait and for pet food. Other species are readily collected in small numbers beneath debris in fields, meadows, and open woodlands. All species of crickets are a good protein source for your lizards.

Gray crickets are so inexpensive that few hobbyists breed them. If you need only a few, they can be purchased from local pet shops. If you are feeding numerous insectivorous lizards, purchase your crickets from wholesale producers that advertise in fishing or reptile magazines. Prices are quite reasonable when crickets are purchased in multiples of 1,000.

This is a hatchling of the black-throated morph of the white-throated monitor.

Mealworms and cockroaches should be part of a healthy monitor and tegu diet.

Feed your crickets a good varied diet and sprinkle the food with calcium/vitamin D3 for the benefit of the lizards to which the crickets are fed. Crickets are cannibalistic if crowded or underfed. Although they are able to metabolize most of their moisture requirements from fruit and vegetables, they will also appreciate a water source. Crickets will drown easily if they are given a plain, shallow dish of water. Instead, lean a small stick against the inside edge of the water container as a ladder or place cotton balls, a sponge, or even pebbles or aquarium gravel in the water dish. These will give the crickets sufficient purchase to climb out when they fall in.

Keep crumpled newspapers, the tubes from rolls of paper towels, or other such hiding areas in the crickets' cage. We prefer paper towel tubes, for they can be lifted and the requisite number of crickets shaken from inside them into the cage or a transportation jar. This makes it easier to handle the fast-moving, agile insects. A tightly covered 20-gallon (76-L) tank will temporarily house 1,000 crickets. Provide a substrate of sawdust, soil, vermiculite, or other such medium. This must be changed often to prevent excessive odor from the insects.

Grasshoppers/locusts (*Locusta* sp. and *Shistocerca* sp. in part): Although these are migratory and other locusts are not available in the United States, they are widely used as reptile foods in European and Asian countries. These can be bred or collected. Grasshoppers can be field collected in the United States by the deft wielding of a field net. However, grasshoppers are fast and may be difficult to collect.

Caution: In some southern areas large, slow grasshoppers called *lubbers* may be found. Many of these have a brightly colored (often black and yellow or red) nymphal stage that can be fatally toxic if eaten. The tan and buff adults seem to be less toxic, but their use as a food item is not suggested.

Waxworms (*Galleria* sp.): The "waxworm" is really the caterpillar, the larval stage of the wax moth that frequently infests neglected beehives. These are available commercially from many sources and are ideal food for small monitors and dwarf tegus. Check the ads in any reptile and amphibian magazine for wholesale distributors. Some pet shops and bait shops also carry waxworms. If you buy wholesale quantities of waxworms, you will need to feed them. Chick laying mash, wheat germ, honey, and yeast mixed into a syrupy paste will serve adequately as the diet for these insects.

Giant mealworms (*Zoophobas* sp.): These are the larvae of a South American beetle. They are rather new in the herpetocultural trade and at

CAUTION: Do not feed your lizards roaches from areas or habitations where insecticides are used!

A hatchling Dumeril's monitor explores its cage.

present, their ready availability is being threat-ened in the United States by the Department of Agriculture. This is unfortunate, for Zoophobas have proved to be of great value to reptile breeders.

Although they are still available in many areas of the United States and virtually all over Europe and Asia, it would seem prudent for American herpetoculturists to breed their own.

Zoophobas can be kept in quantity in shallow plastic trays containing an inch (2.5 cm) or so of sawdust. To breed these mealworms, place one in each of a series of empty film canisters or other similar small containers that contain some sawdust, bran, or oats. The containment tends to induce pupation. After a few days the worm will pupate, eventually metamorphosing into a fair-sized black beetle. The beetles can be placed together for egg laying in a plastic tub

HELPFUL HINT: The mealworms will obtain all of their moisture requirements from the fresh vegetables and fruit.

containing a sawdust substrate and some old cracked limbs and twigs. The female beetles deposit their eggs in the cracks in the limbs. The beetles and their larvae can be fed vegeta-bles, fruits, oats, and bran.

You can keep two colonies rotating to assure that you have all sizes of the larvae you will need to offer your various monitors and tegus. Although giant mealworms seem more easily digested by the lizards than common meal-worms, neither species should be fed exclusively.

Mealworms (*Tenebrio molitor*): Long a favorite of neophyte reptile and amphibian keepers, mealworms should be just a part of your lizard's diet. These insects are easily kept and bred in plastic receptacles containing bran for food (available at your local livestock feed store). A potato or an apple will supply needed moisture.

Roaches: Although these can be bred, it is nearly as easy to collect roaches as needed if you can avoid areas where pesticides are used. Roaches, of one or more species, are present over much of the world. Commercial breeders often concentrate on such large and "exotic" roach species as the Madagascar hissing and the tropical American giant. The size of the roach proffered must be tailored to the size of the lizard being fed.

Mice and Rats: To Purchase or Breed

Both mice and rats may be purchased—either alive or prekilled—from pet shops and/or commercial rodent breeders. We prefer to purchase the rodents we need prekilled and frozen in bulk lots. Rodent suppliers often advertise in the classified sections of the various reptile and amphibian magazines. Local herpetology clubs, museums, nature centers, or biology departments may be able to direct you to local commercial sources. Do remember that it is much less costly to ship frozen rodents than to ship live ones.

Mice are easily bred. A single male to two or three females in a 10-gallon (38-L) tank (or rodent-breeding cage) will produce a steady supply of babies that can be fed to your growing monitor, tegus, and their relatives. When you set up the caging, do not use cedar bedding as a substrate. It may smell nice to you, but those aromatic phenols are inhaled by your rodents and are unhealthy for them and for the animals that feed upon them. We suggest that you use aspen (our first choice) or pine shavings.

Feed your rodents either a "lab chow" diet that is specifically formulated for them or a healthful mixture of seeds and vegetables. No other kibble-type diet is advised for your rodents. Fresh water must be present at all times.

Except that their caging should be larger, rats can be raised in much the same manner as mice.

Large roaches, like this one, should be fed to large lizards.

Rats do not breed as quickly as mice, and take longer to mature. Rats are an excellent staple (but not exclusive) food for larger monitors.

Vitamin/Mineral Supplements

Even with a well-rounded diet, it unquestionably is best to occasionally supplement your lizard's diet with vitamin/mineral additives. Those supplements most recommended supply calcium at a ratio of at least two to one over phosphorus, written like this: 2:1. Vitamin D3 is also an important additive, but administer only very small amounts; an excess of vitamin D3 in your reptile's diet can be detrimental.

Vitamin D3 is essential to reptiles and amphibians. D3 aids in the metabolizing of calcium. Although reptiles can make their own vitamin D3 if allowed access to natural sunlight, lack of UVB means you'll need to add D3 to the diet. The fluorescent bulbs labeled "full spectrum" won't trigger vitamin D3 production. Even if you use a UVA/UVB incandescent bulb such as UVHeat, you may wish to add calcium to the diet.

Exactly how much calcium is necessary remains speculative. Rapidly growing baby and immature lizards most certainly have a higher calcium requirement than adults. Specimens recovering from rickets or metabolic bone disease will need more calcium than healthy specimens. Phosphorus is almost always amply present in the normal diet of captive lizards, so many experienced and successful keepers and breeders recommend the augmentation of the calcium alone. At our facility we have used both the additives that supply only calcium and vitamin D3 and additives containing a broader spectrum of ingredients. We can fault neither nor recommend one more strongly over the other.

Several excellent calcium additives are available at both your pet store and your veterinarian. The vitamin/mineral supplements that we have used over the years are Osteo-Form and Rep-Cal. Osteo-Form (calcium and phosphorus with vitamins) is a product of Vet-A-Mix, Inc. of Shenandoah, Iowa; it contains about twice as much calcium as phosphorus. Osteo-Form also contains a high amount of vitamin A and lesser amounts of vitamin D3 and vitamin C. Although this product contains more vitamin A than many herpetoculturists prefer, we have been very happy with the results. It is usually available from veterinarians, feed stores, and some pet shops. Rep-Cal is calcium and vitamin D3 with no phosphorus. It is a product of Rep-Cal Research Labs of Los Gatos, California.

Dosage: How much should you offer and how frequently? For adults, meaning those longer than three feet (1 m), add a pinch of

the powder over their food twice weekly. For rapidly growing younger lizards add a small pinch of the powdered vitamin daily.

Watering and Hydration Techniques

Some monitors get large. By large, we mean those monitors in the size range of the Nile and Asian—those that attain or exceed 6 feet (2 m) in length and are heavy of body. To be even relatively comfortable, these big lizards need a bathtub-sized water receptacle. Some specimens that are particularly large in either length or girth may be severely constrained even in a water container of this size. Because monitors are of tropical and subtropical origin, their water, no matter the volume, should be warm. We have found 80–85°F (27–30°C) to be suitable.

How do you drain, sterilize, and refill a bathtub-sized water receptacle? Truthfully, this can become an arduous task, and one you must do daily to keep the water container even moderately clean. The water must be kept warm enough for the lizard, about 78–84°F (25–29°C), difficult and expensive to do in a container of this size.

The good news is that some species, such as the savanna and white-throated monitors, will do quite well with just a sizable dish of drinking water and an occasional swim in your bathtub. But access to a large water container or pool water should always be provided for water-oriented monitor species.

Water dishes should be available at all times for all species of monitors and tegus. Even desert forms that in nature may not have the opportunity to drink every day, will, when captive, drink frequently and copiously.

HELPFUL HINT: Monitors and tegus having unlimited access to natural unfiltered sunlight will not require as many vitamin/mineral supplements as will those lizards maintained under artificial lighting.

Half in, half out: This red tegu will soon emerge completely.

Misting: Persistently arboreal species may prefer to drink from the droplets on freshly misted leaves. For these, misting should be done daily. This is especially important in combating dehydration in newly imported and stressed representatives of particularly slender monitor species that come from humid forested habitats. Among these are the emerald and black tree monitors. When you mist, aim the mister up, so the water falls down onto the leaves and the lizard. Make sure that the slender hatchlings of Asian water, Nile, and other monitor species that originate from riparian habitats have enough access to water, both for drinking and for swimming.

Keeping the provided water clean and the receptacle cleanable is as important as actually providing the water. Although the cleaning of the small water bowl needed to accommodate a baby monitor is relatively simple, keeping a clean water supply for a 7-foot-long (2.1-m), beer-keg diameter Asian water monitor is a whole different story. Necessarily, the container is immense, the volume of water is great, and if the monitor has defecated in it, cleaning is difficult. The most satisfactory method of draining and refilling large containers of water is to have them plumbed into the home water and drainage systems. Although the initial expense may be considerable, over time you will truly appreciate the convenience. The alternative is a frequent changing, pail by pail, followed by a difficult-to-accomplish sterilizing, rinsing, and refilling.

> **HELPFUL HINT:** All water dishes should be secured in place. This will prevent a boisterous monitor from overturning the dish, a feat at which they are particularly adept.

Watering Techniques for Tegus

Tegus are terrestrial. They require no more than a shallow drinking container of suitable size. None of the tegus is prone to taking the long soaks that typify so many of the monitors. In contrast to the tegus, however, the caiman lizards are found in riverine situations. From slowly moving, heavily vegetated water, these large lizards often crawl out onto mats of emergent vegetation, overhanging trees, and riverine debris to bask and dry. Captives appreciate and fully use large water tubs. If the water is of sufficient depth, caiman lizards may

Hatchling mangrove monitors are very brightly colored.

submerge for long periods—sometimes days—occasionally tipping their snouts upward through the surface to breathe.

Hydration Chamber

If you acquire a monitor or tegu that is dehydrated, you may need to offer more than a clean water dish. A hydration chamber may be the answer. Although the name sounds elaborate, the hydration chamber is nothing more than a rain chamber.

The prompt use of a hydration chamber can make the difference between life and death for freshly imported, slender, easily dehydrated species such as the emerald and black tree monitors. What they need is a week or so of warm, natural rains and high humidity to help stabilize and rehydrate them. What you can

provide is almost as good—a humid enclosure and periodic mistings.

Making your own: A small hydration chamber can be constructed of wire mesh over a wood frame (an "open" system), or you can use an aquarium, partially filled with water and equipped with a circulating water pump and a wire mesh top, for a "closed" system.

If you are fortunate enough to live in a warm climate, the wire mesh cage containing the lizard can be moved outdoors, a mist nozzle screwed onto the end of a garden hose and affixed over the cage, and fresh water "rain" run through the cage for an hour or more a day.

If you need to set up the system indoors, the wire cage can be placed on top of or inside a properly draining utility tub and a spray nozzle added to the faucet. The nozzle is placed atop

The yellow tree monitor is alert, small, and agile.

the wire cage and tepid water is sprayed through the cage for an hour or so. Keep an eye on the sink if you use this setup; if the drain somehow clogs up, the sink will quickly overflow. A secondary (backup) drain (just in case. . .) might do much to guarantee your peace of mind.

In closed systems, the lizard is placed atop a wire mesh "table" that keeps the animal 2 inches (5 cm) or so above the water in the bottom of the aquarium. A recirculating pump in the water underneath the lizard pumps the water up into a small-diameter PVC pipe that's placed atop the mesh tank top. The PVC pipe has a series of lateral holes drilled along its length, and the far end is capped. The water drips through the holes in the PVC down into the tank, creating a "rain chamber" that recirculates.

It is imperative that the water in self-contained systems be kept immaculately clean and lukewarm; if the lizard defecates into the water, change the water immediately.

Gould's monitor is a large and alert Australian desert species.

HANDLING

"Tame" monitors and tegus may not always remain so as they mature, and they may use claws, teeth, and tail to discourage your advances.

Many monitors and tegus can become tame and trustworthy if obtained at a young age and given careful, gentle, and persistent handling. At one herpetological meeting we attended, a young lady arrived toting under one arm one of the biggest savanna monitors we had ever seen, and under the other arm what was certainly the largest black and white tegu we had ever seen. She had had both from babies nad expended oodles of care and affection on the animals, and the results were gratifying.

Some species tend to tame more readily than others, but some examples of even the more traditionally irascible species will become tame. Of the monitors, the African savanna and the Asian water monitor tame rather readily. The first of these two is perhaps the most common monitor in the pet store trade; the latter was once commonly seen, but is no longer so.

A Timor monitor in its habitat.

The African Nile monitor, a very pretty black and yellow species that is still common in the pet trade, has a well-deserved reputation for being one of the more difficult species to tame. Although some babies do tame, most remain flighty and ready to bite. If they are larger than hatchling size when imported from the wild, they are even more difficult to tame.

Of the tegus, the Amazonian black and yellow, the species most commonly available, is also the most difficult to tame. The larger black and white and the red tegus are comparatively easygoing animals but are expensive and available only occasionally from specialty dealers.

Monitors and tegus that are unaccustomed to handling have a remarkable set of defensive tactics to advise you that they much prefer to be left alone. Not all of the tactics are used by all species (some seem not to slap with their tails, for instance), but those mechanisms that are used may be used singly or in combination.

A subadult Komodo dragon, V. komodoensis, shows more color than the adults.

When acquired young and handled frequently and gently, some monitors become very tame, even allowing themselves to be walked on a leash like this savanna monitor.

HELPFUL HINT: Thick gloves and a long-sleeved shirt will provide you with a certain advantage when beginning your taming efforts with any sizable monitor or tegu.

Body Language

Monitors first rely on escape to avoid enemies, either real or imagined. If, however, they are cornered and unable to flee, body language—intimidation of an enemy through posturing that includes laterally flattening and arcing the body, expanding the throat, and lolling the tongue out—is the next line of defense. During this, the tail is often arced and lashed with unerring accuracy. This may seem ludicrous when it is indulged in by a small monitor, but it is no laughing matter when the tail of a large monitor connects with your hand, arm, leg, or—if you happen to be bending toward the lizard—your face.

Like monitors, tegus would prefer flight to confrontation with enemies. However, if cornered, tegus tend to inflate their bodies, arc them upward, and inflate their throats. They bite (very effectively), scratch (less effectively than many monitors), and void their intestinal contents on a captor, but tend not to slap with their tails.

Biting

This sounds straightforward enough. Not all monitor species are predisposed to biting when

The 10-inch length of the Asian water monitor, V. salvator, *gives little indication that the lizard may be close to 8 feet long when adult.*

handled. The smaller species tend to be the least aggressive. Even if they were to bite you, they aren't big enough to hurt you.

The damage potential goes up when you get to the fairly small monitors, the green and black tree monitors. They have a snout–vent length (SVL) of only about 10 inches (25 cm), but they are perfectly ready to bite when disturbed; hold on with bulldog tenacity once they have you in their mouth, and will clamp down more tightly at every movement you make to extricate yourself. You can be hurt—and hurt badly.

If a fairly small monitor can do this sort of damage, you absolutely don't want to get

bitten by one of the larger monitor species. Coupled with the power of the bite is the worry that the teeth and jaws of many monitor species may carry substantial quantities of bacteria. This is especially so if the lizard has been feeding on well-ripened carrion. Wash and disinfect any bite wounds carefully and thoroughly, and seek medical attention for the infection that is very likely to follow.

Wild tegus bite readily and hard when cornered, but often do not retain their grip with the tenacity of a monitor. We have never had a tegu fail to release its grip when it was placed upon the ground.

Although some do tame, ornate monitors, **V. ornatus,** *are not a pet species for everyone.*

Scratching: Again, this behavior sounds straightforward, but with many monitor species it is anything but simple. A carelessly grasped monitor, especially an arboreal type with sharply recurved claws, will display a talent at raking with its claws that is sure to amaze the first-time recipient of the technique.

Unless prevented from doing so, when grasped and resting in your arms, a monitor will twist its ventral surface against your arm, spread its rear legs wide to tightly grasp your arm, then dig in its claws deliberately and rake the skin on your arm.

Put the monitor gently back into its cage, and close and secure the door/top. Wash and disinfect the welts and wounds carefully and

HELPFUL HINT: A tegu's tail can auto-tomize and regenerate, to a degree. If a monitor's tail is broken, it does not regenerate.

The Australian lace monitor, V. varius, has only recently become available to hobbyists.

thoroughly! Monitor claws can transmit bacteria to the wounds.

The claws of the largely terrestrial tegus are not strongly recurved. Tegus can and will scratch their captors in their attempts to escape, but are less effective in these efforts than many monitors.

Voiding the contents of the intestinal tract: Many monitors are not at all reluctant to add insult to injury. While they are biting you or raking you with their claws, leaving welts or bleeding scratches, these lizards may also void a copious amount of fluid and feces from their intestinal tracts. At best this is harmless but messy, smelly, and disconcerting! However, it can also cause infection if it enters an open wound. In all cases, thoroughly wash and disinfect your hands, arms, and additional splashed areas of your body. If you are in doubt, consult a physician.

Although a frightened, carelessly restrained tegu will void, these lizards are less apt to do so than most monitors.

Behavior after exposure to natural sunlight: Owners who have raised and tamed their monitors and tegus indoors under artificial lighting *may* see a dramatic change for the worse in the attitude of their lizards when they are exposed to natural sunlight.

Not all of these lizards become aggressive when in natural sunlight, and all will revert to their former state of complacency (if applicable) when moved back indoors.

Some of these lizards (tegus, especially) may be most savage during the breeding season, and females are often especially so as the egg deposition date nears.

To a degree, you can consider the feistiness shown by a freshly imported monitor or tegu a barometer of the lizard's overall health. If a newly imported monitor or tegu does not respond defensively to your overtures, it is probably a sick or weak lizard that you should not consider purchasing. In most cases, with lizards in these two groupings, belligerence equates, to some degree, with stamina and health.

A fully warmed monitor or tegu will be more difficult to approach and handle than a cool or cold specimen, simply because warmed specimens move more quickly and decisively. A monitor or tegu warmed by natural, unfiltered sunlight will be more difficult yet. However, an optimally warmed monitor is more apt to try to escape than to bite. The reverse will often be true of a cool/cold monitor or tegu. As if recognizing that its suboptimal body temperature will cause it to be slower and less agile, a cool monitor or tegu is more apt to stand its ground, jaws gaping, in biting readiness.

How does one handle such an animal—an animal that will wriggle, squirm, bite, and scratch when grasped? The basic response must be "carefully—very carefully!"

The body and neck of very small wild specimens can be encircled with the fingers of one hand.

The head should be immobilized in the same manner as you would immobilize the head of a snake.

Larger wild monitors and tegus require a coordinated two-handed capture technique. With one hand you should encircle the neck, the head, and the forelimbs while simultaneously immobilizing the rear limbs with the other hand. It would be best if the tail could be immobilized with a third hand, but lacking this appendage, grasping the tail between your arm and body may save you some welts, or at least some discomfort. Tail immobilization is more important with large monitors than with tegus.

Even when handling large monitors and tegus that seem perfectly tame, always watch for signs of irascibility, especially if handling or husbandry techniques are changed. Being prepared for any eventuality may well save you from an uncomfortable encounter.

Merely handling your monitor or tegu is very different from trying to tame it. If you hope to tame the lizard, we strongly suggest that you begin with the youngest specimen available and work with it—preferably several times daily. Select one of the more easily tamed species, and if you have your choice of several similar ones, choose a healthy-appearing, relatively nonaggressive individual. When nearing or handling your lizard, always move slowly and nonthreateningly.

V. dumerilii.

If your lizard will allow you to touch it without threatening to bite, do so without gloves. If it is more aggressive, wear gloves, even if they are thin. Your hope is to gradually accustom your lizard to being touched, lifted, and carried. You may choose to first merely rub its nape or dorsum gently. When the lizard tires of this, it will inflate its body or dash away. Desist, then try again in an hour or two. Next, gently lift the lizard. Grasp it tightly enough so it can't squirm free, but not so tightly that it feels incapacitated and threatened. Next allow it to walk from hand to hand, holding the lizard close enough to a horizontal surface so if it falls or jumps it will not hurt itself. Go through the same procedure day after day, several times a day if possible.

Eventually most monitors will lose their fear of you, and you will be able to handle them easily. However, there are always the few that will resist your most persistent and gentle overtures and simply remain nervous and untrusting. If you can be satisfied with a nonhandleable monitor or tegu, keep and enjoy the lizard. If not, divest yourself of it and begin the process anew.

A word of caution: Not everyone likes lizards—especially large lizards. The pathway to regulations and restrictions is often opened when someone is frightened by an unthinking or uncaring monitor or tegu owner. People who do not wish to encounter these animals have that right. Adverse interactions can only lead to additional regulatory laws. Be a responsible pet owner. Use care and courtesy at all times.

Regulations about the ownership of large reptiles may already be in effect in your community. Care and be aware.

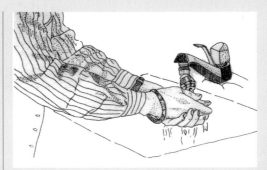

Hands should be washed thoroughly after handling a lizard.

Holding a tame white-throated monitor.

Once in your home, your monitor or tegu will rarely be exposed to pathogens, but an improper diet can cause serious health problems.

Diet-Related Health Problems

Although varanids and teiids seem less prone than many lizards to diet-related health problems, they can and do occur. All can be avoided (and sometimes corrected) by providing a correct diet.

The four most commonly encountered problems are metabolic bone disease (including rickets and demineralization), liver dysfunction, vitamin/mineral imbalance, and elimination problems (constipation or diarrhea).

Our discussion of these problems is in no way intended to supplant the diagnoses and treatments offered by your qualified reptile veterinarian. A qualified reptile veterinarian can be your best friend during times of trouble. The veterinarian's recommendations should be followed to the letter.

Note the bright eyes and attentive look of this baby ornate monitor.

Metabolic Bone Disease (MBD)

In simplified terms, MBD is the withdrawal of bone calcium to maintain the needed level of calcium in the blood. The cause is improper diet, and yes, it is entirely preventable.

A lizard suffering from MBD is usually inactive and, except for a plumpness in its limbs, appears thin. Sometimes the jawbones become shortened and the face looks chubby. That "plumpness" is your cue. It signifies a major health problem, that the calcium is being leached from the bony tissue and replaced by a fibrous tissue. Your animal needs immediate veterinary care.

The technical names for metabolic bone disease are *nutritional secondary hyperparathyroidism* and *fibrous osteodystrophy.* Common names for the problem include rickets and demineralization. The disease is most commonly seen in lizards that have been fed a diet rich in phosphorus and deficient in calcium or that are unable to properly absorb and metabolize their calcium because of a lack of vitamin D3.

The precise markings of hatchling savanna monitors will fade with age.

To exist, your monitor or tegu needs a certain level of blood calcium. When the level of blood calcium drops below a certain percentage, the parathyroid glands begin the complex process of withdrawing calcium from the bones to the blood. As the bones lose their rigidity, parts become replaced with a fibrous tissue and deformities occur. The lizard becomes inactive because its weakened bones won't support its weight.

The preventive agent for MBD is calcium, offered in a ratio of two parts calcium to one part phosphorus.

Your lizard also needs vitamin D3 in order to absorb the calcium. This may be in the form of vitamin D3 supplements, especially when your specimen does not have regular (daily, or at least weekly) access to direct unfiltered sunlight or to light from one of the UVHeat-type bulbs.

Lizards with unlimited access to natural unfiltered sunlight require a lesser amount of D3 and calcium additive than those with limited or no such access. Regular vitamin/mineral augmentation of the diet is very important.

Even when a diet provides sufficient calcium, MBD will occur if the phosphorus ratio is too high or vitamin D3 is not present. The debilitation is a long process through which your lizard will often continue eating and reacting "normally" until it is no longer able to do so.

MBD can be treated by the injections of a soluble calcium and vitamin D3. The treatment will work for MBD in its early stages and in some late-stage cases.

The treatment begins with lab work to determine the actual blood calcium levels. Once the diagnosis of MBD is confirmed, your veterinarian will begin three days of treatment with injectable calcium and (often) oral vitamin D3. Oral calcium may also be administered.

Once the calcium level has been corrected, a supplemented diet (and UV light) will help your lizard maintain its health.

Vitamin/Mineral Imbalances

Throughout this text, we have stressed the importance of vitamins and minerals in correct proportions. Because this aspect is critically important, we will stress it again here.

1. Calcium is necessary for proper bone development and life itself. Ultraviolet rays promote vitamin D3 synthesis and allow reptiles to properly absorb and metabolize calcium. Natural sunlight is the best source for UV, but a UVA/UVB incandescent bulb is a good substitute.

2. Vitamin D3 is necessary to help a reptile absorb and metabolize the necessary amounts of calcium. Too much D3 will allow too much calcium to be absorbed; too little D3 will retard calcium absorption.

3. Phosphorus, when offered at too high a level, can hinder the proper metabolizing of calcium.

4. Vitamin A is usually present in adequate amounts in your lizard's normal diet. Vitamin A enhancements are seldom necessary.

5. Vitamin B is usually of no concern in carnivorous lizards eating a varied diet. Thiamine (B1) imbalances (which cause nerve disorders) could occur if a preponderance of dead fish is fed. If detected early, this disorder is usually correctable.

6. Vitamin C is synthesized internally and also adequately present in balanced diets. A deficiency would manifest itself in hemorrhaging of the mucous membranes and bruising.

7. Vitamin D: The integral role of vitamin D3 in the health of your lizard has already been discussed in detail.

8. Vitamin E deficiencies are diet related. A healthy, varied diet will assure that no vitamin E deficiencies occur.

Constipation and Diarrhea

The normal bowel movements of varanids and teiids vary remarkably in consistency. Normal movements are largely white with some dark coloration. The white portions are urinary solid wastes, called urates. The dark brown portions are feces. Those of a properly hydrated lizard will be moist, like a semiliquid jelly. Those of dehydrated specimens will be dry.

Bowel movements do not necessarily occur at regular intervals. Cooler lizards will defecate less frequently than specimens kept at warmer temperatures.

If a monitor or tegu is kept too cool, the digestive process may either stop or be so inhibited that ingested foods spoil in the stomach. In extreme cases, the lizard may vomit these masses. Properly warm temperatures are mandatory for normal digestive processes to occur. An ideal daytime temperature range would be between 86 and 94°F (30–34°C). Slightly cooler daytime temperatures from 77 to 80°F (25–27°C) are permissible for short periods.

The failure of your lizard to defecate or pass urates may also result from a gastrointestinal impaction. The chances of this are heightened in monitors and tegus that are grossly overweight or very inactive. Impactions may be caused by ingested matter (pebbles, shavings, or kitty litter), or by abnormally dry stools (in

HELPFUL HINT: You lizard's body temperature will largely determine the speed with which digestion occurs.

dehydrated teiids). Again, proper hydration will preclude many problems.

A period of activity, such as a swim in a tub of tepid water, may induce defecation. Large immovable impactions may require veterinary intervention. Some impactions may respond to small amounts of softening agents or lubricants available from your pharmacy. Use milk of magnesia or Siblin—administered orally—or small amounts of petroleum jelly inserted rectally.

Fecal material that is not expelled has more and more moisture reabsorbed, and then normal bowel peristaltic motility cannot expel it. These stubborn impactions may require surgical removal.

Diarrhea is a condition in which your lizards produce abnormally loose stools. Occasional loose stools may be caused by a dietary change, in tegus, by the ingestion of moisture-laden fruit, by periods of stress, illness, or other such abnormal conditions. In most cases, this is nothing to worry about. Cutting back on fruit and/or adding items with a lower fat content will likely correct the looseness.

Intestinal worms and overgrowth of some species of gut bacteria can also cause diarrhea. Veterinary intervention is indicated in either case. The worms should be eradicated. The bacteria count can be lowered via antibiotic administration.

Mechanical Injury

Despite your every caution, monitors and tegus may sustain an injury. The lizards may find undreamed-of ways to lodge themselves against a heating lamp and get burned; a metal staple may break off and the lizard may be cut or punctured by the jagged edge; or the lizard may get injured in the shipping process en route to the pet store. With animals, as with small children, you can adopt a corollary of Murphy's Law: They can get hurt when you least expect it. This section will help you deal with some of the more common traumatic incidents, such as burns, cuts, abrasions, rubbed noses, injured toes, clipping toenails, broken limbs, and skin-shedding problems.

Burns: Your captive lizard can be burned in any of several ways. The most frequent cause is prolonged contact with a cage heating or lighting element that is either malfunctioning or for which proper protection has not been installed.

Among others, "hot rocks," other heating units, and incandescent lightbulbs have been implicated in superficial to severe burning incidents. Burned areas are often discolored but are usually not blistered. Treatment depends upon the severity of the burn. Superficial burns often require no treatment at all, but the cause must be corrected. Mild to moderate burns must be cleaned and antiseptic ointment applied, especially if the burn is oozing fluid. Severe burns need vigorous medical treatment; your veterinarian should be consulted immediately. One of the problems you will have to deal with will be the lizard's loss of appetite, combined with a great need for fluids and energy/calories for healing.

We are not proponents of hot rocks, heat bricks, or other similar ventrally oriented heating devices. Most monitors and tegus are heliotherms (basking species) that preferentially thermoregulate by basking in the sunlight until warm. They then move to a more shaded area so as not to overheat. They are designed to absorb and evenly distribute warmth through their bodies most efficiently when heated from above. This should not be construed as meaning

Baby Gould's monitors are occasionally available.

that on cloudy days, or even at other times when they are cool, they will not happily rest on a warmed surface. They will! But we—and often they—think that dorsal is better. It is for this reason that they regularly and readily use a lighted area warmed by a heat bulb.

Heat and other incandescent bulbs need to be carefully placed, too. A high-wattage, heat-emitting bulb that is too close can burn.

If you are convinced that a ventral heater is necessary, we most readily recommend under-tank heaters.

Cuts and abrasions may be as diverse in severity as burns. The seriousness of either determines the needed response. The cause of the injury needs to be corrected immediately. If the wound is dirty, clean it with soap and water; be sure to rinse well. For a minimal wound an over-the-counter antiseptic ointment will suffice. As with humans, if possible, the area needs to be protected from dirt until it heals. The problem is that commercial strip bandages either won't stick to lizard skin or they stick too well and are hard to remove. Depending on where the injury is, you might be able to wrap a gauze bandage around the affected area and secure the bandage to itself with adhesive tape. A product called New Skin may work better than a bandage for mild cuts and abrasions. For more serious wounds, veterinary assistance should be sought immediately.

Nose rubbing is one of the most common abrasions and one of the most difficult to correct. It is the direct result of your lizard's escape efforts and may be indulged in by either tame or wild specimens. It makes little difference to the lizards whether the cage is constructed of glass or wire (is smooth or rough).

HELPFUL HINT: A monitor or tegu that has been burned needs about twice its normal calorie intake every day—but it may have no appetite at all.

Tongue extended, this black tree monitor explores its enclosure.

Nose rubbing by newly collected monitors and tegus or by specimens that have been used to "the run of the house" is self-explanatory. Nose rubbing by fearful wild lizards that are trying unsuccessfully to return to the wild is equally easily explained. Larger cages may lessen the problem by providing a greater feeling of security and more actual "freedom."

Covering at least three sides of the cage with opaque paper, cloth, or Contact paper may also help alleviate the problem.

To prevent easily startled, extremely wild specimens from repeatedly reinjuring their snouts, it may be necessary to cover the remaining side as well. However, in truth this is self-defeating, for it will prevent the lizards from ever becoming accustomed to motion and your presence. Another method, one that we prefer for extremely wild specimens, is to suspend a soft cloth barrier about 2 inches (5 cm) on the inside of the glass or wire sides of the cage. By coming in contact with the hanging cloth first, the specimen substantially lessens its impact with the cage side. For the side that you approach most frequently, the barricade can be suspended halfway up from the bottom. This way, the lizard can see you and yet avoid injury if it runs into the cage wall.

Toe problems: Broken toes, torn-off toenails, and sharp claws are all frequently encountered when one keeps lizards. Toes may be broken during escape efforts, or the lizard may snag its claws inextricably in carpeting or in a narrow aperture. Sometimes humans step on the toe of an uncaged monitor or tegu.

If the break is fresh and simple, the toe often

may be splinted and saved. If the break is old and/or compound, amputation is usually preferred. Consult your veterinarian.

Torn-off toenails occur for the same series of reasons as breaks. Apply an antiseptic ointment or powder, and keep your lizard quiet until the bleeding stops. These injuries often heal quickly without any additional procedures. However, if the toe becomes swollen or infected, consult your veterinarian.

Many monitors and some tegus are partially to extensively arboreal. To accommodate their climbing habits, their claws are sharp and curved.

In the wild, the lizard's normal activity usually keeps the claws somewhat shortened and dulled. Because most captive monitors or tegus never have the opportunity to climb and run extensively, you may need to occasionally clip **off** the very tip of the claw. Often a two-person job, nail trimming is easiest (especially if the lizard is large) if the specimen is firmly but gently restrained and rolled onto its side with its belly facing the person who is to do the trimming. Using either human or pet nail clippers, it is then possible to carefully remove the tip of the claw. If the claws of baby lizards are carefully inspected, you can often see traces of venation at their cores. Care should be taken not to cut the claw so short that it bleeds. If bleeding does occur, apply a styptic and an antibiotic powder or salve.

Occasionally a constriction of thread or even unshed skin on the toe can inhibit normal blood circulation. If unresolved, this can lead to the distal portion blackening as the tissue dies, dries out, and eventually drops off. Normally this is not accompanied by any swelling or infection, and, in fact, is seldom detected until

it is too late to correct the problem. A periodic inspection of your lizard's toes for constricting fibers or rings of dried skin and their prompt and gentle removal if found can lessen the probability of a problem.

Broken tail: The breaking of a tail is of different severity when it happens to a monitor than when it happens to a teiid.

Monitors have no fracture planes in the caudal vertebrae, and their tail will not regenerate if broken. The tail break may heal if splinted, or it may be necessary to have the tail amputated. Consult your veterinarian.

Although the breaking of a tail in an otherwise perfect teiid lizard can be disheartening, it is probably considered more serious by the keeper than the kept. The tails of teiid lizards are designed by Mother Nature to break if necessary. This is a defensive mechanism with considerable survival value. In some of the caudal (tail) vertebrae there is a weakened "fracture plane" to facilitate easy breakage. If, as frequently happens, a predator grasps the lizard by the tail, the tail breaks off, and through convulsive wriggling, retains the predator's attention. Unless the break is well up on the basal portion of the tail, little bleeding accompanies the autotomization. Regeneration of the tail begins nearly immediately.

The completeness and appearance of the regenerated tail depends upon numerous criteria. Among others are the age of the lizard, the area of the break, and whether or not the break was clean and complete or irregular and partial.

Tails broken beyond the center point of the tail usually regenerate more completely than those broken closer to the body. A clean, complete break usually results in a more normally tapering, natural-appearing regenerated member. With care (and luck) a partial break may heal in a natural position. Alternatively, the break may complete itself at a later date and heal askew; in some cases a second, abnormal-appearing tail may grow to join the first.

Tails of young teiids broken on their distal half seldom need attention. Tails of adults broken on their distal third are likewise not apt to require attention. The tails of both young and old broken closer to the body may require cauterization and/or suturing to stanch blood flow and quickly close the wound.

In all cases, clean the break with a dilute Betadine solution and keep the area clean.

Broken limbs: The leg bones of monitors and tegus are strong and designed to withstand considerable stress without mishap. In the wild, one of these lizards with a broken limb would be easy prey. Arboreal monitors have been seen dropping several dozen feet from a tree limb where they were basking to both dry ground and water. After landing on the former they scuttled off at great speed, showing no evidence that the drop had affected them adversely. When landing in water they dive and swim to safety, again showing no ill effects from the powerful landing impact.

Therefore, if a captive monitor or tegu breaks its leg, it is usually either caused by an accident or indicative of another underlying problem such as metabolic bone disease (see page 39). In either case, your veterinarian will splint and/or surgically pin the limb.

If the break was caused by an accident, steps should be taken to ascertain that it does not have an opportunity to recur. If the break was the result of calcium deficiency, the lizard will need to have its calcium level improved via injectable calcium, and then dietary corrections must immediately be made.

Infections: If kept in clean caging, neither monitors nor tegus are likely to develop infections, even from open wounds. It is when their quarters are allowed to become dirty or when the animals are stressed that infections are most likely to occur. If untreated, infections can literally and quickly overwhelm even an otherwise healthy specimen.

Abscesses, suppuration, discolorations, and other such abnormal signs may indicate either a localized or a systemic infection. Swollen limbs might mean metabolic bone disease, an equally serious problem covered earlier in this chapter. A veterinarian well versed in reptilian disorders should be consulted immediately.

In some cases it may be necessary to obtain cultures to determine an effective treatment. In other cases the causative agents may respond quickly to broad-spectrum antibiotics (these will usually be injected for immediate action). When a monitor or tegu is profoundly ill, it generally doesn't eat, or will have trouble metabolizing food if it does eat. In all cases proper cleanliness of both lizard and cage are very important for recovery.

Shedding problems: A monitor or tegu that walks around sporting large patches of exfoliating skin is apt to be perceived as a lizard with problems. Such is usually not the case.

Reptiles shed their skin to facilitate growth. This is natural. Unlike snakes, which are well known for their entire, inverted shed skins, most lizards shed their skin less neatly and in a patchwork manner. This, too, is natural—unless the skin adheres tightly and is not lost by the lizard within a day or two. Increasing the humidity in the cage and moistening your lizard's shedding skin will often help. A gentle tug by you on the edges may also help. It is

A shedding Merten's water monitor watches its surroundings.

important, however, that you not remove the flaking skin before it is ready to be removed. The newly forming skin beneath may be damaged if the process is rushed.

Do spend a few moments checking your lizard after each shed. Ascertain that no rings of scales remain on the digits, tail, or elsewhere, where they may then dry and restrict circulation. Should you find such problems, remove the skin gently and promptly. It may be necessary to soak your lizard for a few minutes to promote softening and facilitate easy removal.

Several other diseases and maladies may rarely occur.

Mineralization of internal organs: This is caused by overdosage of calcium, known as *hypercalcemia*. Treatment is both lengthy and expensive and requires about two weeks of monitoring by a veterinarian. Once the disease has been diagnosed and corrected, you'll need to reduce your specimen's calcium and vitamin D3

intake. There is a fine line between too much and not enough calcium and vitamin D3. Untreated or too far advanced, this disease can be fatal.

Hypoglycemia is an abnormal decrease in blood sugar. Stress or pancreatic dysfunction can be the causative agent. The stress factor is correctable; the pancreatic dysfunction, sometimes caused by an insulin-secreting tumor, usually is not.

Pathogens and Parasites

Ectoparasites: External parasites are less problematic to treat than endoparasites. Only ticks are seen with any regularity on monitors and tegus. They feed on the blood of their host.

Ticks are deflated and seedlike when empty, rounded and bladderlike when engorged. It is best if they are removed singly whenever seen. They imbed their mouthparts deeply when feeding, and if the ticks are merely pulled from

The freckled monitor has a dark-tipped tail.

the lizard, the mouthparts may break off in the wound. It is best to first dust the ticks individually with Sevin powder or to rub them with rubbing alcohol, then return a few minutes later and pull them off gently with a pair of tweezers. You can use a pair of the plastic tick-removal tweezers used for dog ticks if your lizard will hold still long enough. These tweezers grasp the engorged tick lightly while you rotate them to "unscrew" the tick from the lizard.

Respiratory Disorders

Although well-acclimated, properly maintained monitors and tegus are not prone to respiratory ailments, stressed new imports, marginally healthy specimens, and those subjected to unnatural periods of cold (especially damp cold) may occasionally be affected with "colds" or pneumonia. Some respiratory conditions may also be associated with depressed immunity brought about by a heavy endoparasite burden.

Respiratory ailments are initially accompanied by sneezing, lethargic demeanor, and unnaturally rapid, often shallow breathing. As the respiratory infection worsens, rasping and bubbling may accompany each of your lizard's breaths. At this stage the infection is often critical and can be fatal.

Basking temperatures must be elevated during treatment, because monitors and tegus are dependent upon outside heat sources for maintaining their metabolic rate.

As soon as a respiratory ailment is suspected, elevate the temperature of your lizard's basking area to about 100°F (37.7°C). Do not elevate the temperature of the entire cage to this level!

The ambient cage temperature should be 88–92°F (31–33°C). If the symptoms of respiratory distress do not greatly lessen within a day or two, do not delay any longer. Call your veterinarian and take your lizard for antibiotic treatment.

There are many "safe" drugs available, but some respiratory illnesses do not respond well to them. The newer aminoglycoside drugs are more effective, but correspondingly more dangerous. There is little latitude in dosage amounts, and the lizard must be well hydrated to ensure against renal (kidney) damage. The injection site for aminoglycosides should be anterior to midbody to assure that the renal-portal system is not compromised. Your veterinarian must be well acquainted with reptilian medicine to assure that the correct decisions are made.

Endoparasites: The presence of internal parasites in wild-caught monitors and tegus is a given. Among others that may be present are roundworms, pinworms, other nematodes, tapeworms, and a whole host of flagellate protozoans. Although many people think that blanket treatment of all imported specimens is a necessity, we think that whether or not the parasites are combated vigorously should depend on the behavior of each individual lizard; indeed, recent work with green iguanas indicates that some internal "parasites" may actually be symbiotic rather than parasitic.

Certainly the problems created by heavy endoparasitic loads in weakened lizards need to be addressed promptly. Because fecal exams will have to be performed to determine what the lizard is actually harboring in its gut, it is best to avail yourself of the services of a reptilian

HELPFUL HINT: The warmer the surroundings, the better able the lizard is to digest its food and fight off diseases or injury.

veterinarian, who will be best qualified to determine when and with what to treat the problem.

However, if the specimen in question is bright-eyed, alert, feeding well, and has a good color, you may wish to forgo an immediate veterinary assessment. Endoparasitic loads can actually diminish if you keep your specimen's cage scrupulously clean, thereby preventing reinfestation.

Gut and tissue strongyloid nematodes may be particularly persistent. To eradicate them often requires a lengthy bout of purges. We have often wondered at what point a treatment becomes more of a burden for a specimen than the parasites actually are. In the case of strongyles, the answer seems to be a toss-up. Although an overload of strongyloid nematodes can cause chronic diarrhea, a small load of these parasites may cause no problems whatsoever. We think the veterinarian should use discrimination in determining whether or not to treat a given specimen.

Simply stated, the treatment for endoparasites involves administering a potentially toxic substance into your lizard's system. Because of this, dosages of the drug(s) must be exact! It is very easy for a layperson unfamiliar with the conversion of the metric doses of medication to overmedicate or undermedicate a specimen. In the first case the result may be fatal. In the latter case the effort will probably have been futile. Again, we strongly suggest you avail yourself of the services of a knowledgeable veterinarian.

BREEDING

Because we know so little about what factors affect breeding, producing young monitors or tegus is more of an art than a science.

All members of both the Varanidae and the teiids are oviparous; they lay eggs. Because of the low percentage of successful breedings (and even lower percentage of successful hatchlings), we know that we have a lot to learn for long-term success with these lizards. Many clutches will go full term, yet the babies will fail to hatch, or of those that do hatch, some will be deformed. This would indicate improper relative humidity and/or temperatures during incubation. Thus, many of the reproductive parameters suggested in both this section and the species accounts are conjectural.

Although successful captive breeding of monitors and tegus often seems to be the "luck of the draw," there are a few things you can do to stack the deck in your favor:
• retaining your specimens in A-1 health—not skinny, not obese, no heavy load of endoparasites

This albino Nile monitor views passing crowds from the corner of its cage.

• suitable caging (from all husbandry aspects) but especially in terms temperature regimen, space, humidity, and lighting
• accurate sexing of your monitors and tegus (not always easy)
• manipulating photoperiods (natural seems best)
• simulating variation in seasonal temperatures, humidity, and rainfall
• introducing a second male to stimulate agonistic (territorial/aggressive) behavior, which, after dominance is determined, often turns to reproductive activity

Important: Do not get discouraged if, after all of your efforts, your lizards fail to breed. Even those monitors and tegus known to be compatible, proven breeders may fail some years. This is especially likely if they are moved from familiar caging or if disturbing alterations are made to existing caging.

Of the comparatively few monitor breedings reported in the United States, most success has been had with monitors maintained year-round

A portrait of the crocodile monitor.

Specifics for inducing breeding in monitors and tegus, when known, are mentioned in the individual species accounts. Many of the monitor breeding parameters mentioned in the species accounts are based on, and extrapolated from, successes with specimens kept in outside facilities. For some monitors, there are no captive-breeding accounts, either inside or out, on which we may rely.

Health

What makes for health and contentment in a monitor? As for any captive lizard, the most insidious and pervasive problem is stress. Stress, which we will define here as "unease," can be physical or psychological. Injury, ill health, incompatibility with other lizards, being too exposed, being too constrained, being too humid, or too arid—or anything else to excess—can cause stress. Serious stress may have an almost instantaneous adverse result, or the result may be as subtle as the stress itself. But it is a very real threat to your lizard's long-term overall health. Stress may manifest itself as a loss of appetite, a continuing flight response, aggressive actions and reactions, cowering, or any other unnatural behavior by your lizard. The cause must be corrected. The correction may be as easy as providing a new or better hiding area, increasing or reducing heat, providing a more suitable basking area, removing a cagemate or placing an opaque barrier between monitor cages, moving the entire cage to a less heavily trafficked area, or altering the relative humidity or lighting. The cause may be complex and truly tax your

in quasi-natural outside facilities. Such caging and maintenance programs are possible in southern Florida, Texas's Lower Rio Grande Valley, and some areas of Arizona and Southern California. In cooler areas, with protection and forethought (and southern exposures), monitors and tegus can be maintained outside seasonally. If maintained indoors, it will be necessary to fulfill all of the parameters already mentioned and to provide sufficient full-spectrum lighting to induce natural behavior. This is not an easy task.

Despite our best efforts to provide the artificial illumination necessary for monitors and tegus maintained indoors, there really is no substitute for natural unfiltered sunlight to stimulate natural (including reproductive) behavior.

> **HELPFUL HINT:** Unless they are healthy and relatively content, it is unlikely that your monitors will even attempt to breed, or if they do breed, that their efforts will be successful.

The endangered Bengal monitor, V. bengalensis, *is captive bred in small numbers.*

ingenuity to determine its origin. Remember always that a stressed monitor cannot be a healthy or content monitor, nor can it correct the problem itself. The solution rests with you.

There are three important and easily assessed aspects of good health:
• suitable weight: neither thin nor obese, although just a little heavy is better than underweight
• freedom from endoparasites
• no respiratory distress

There are, of course, other physical criteria, less overt and more difficult to diagnose, with which time and experience will familiarize you.

Because monitors' reproductive cycling usually involves cooling the lizards for a variable period of time, a full or partial fast during the period of cooling, and other things (discussed later) that can add to an already stressful situation or further complicate existing health problems, we suggest that you not even try to cycle a monitor with known health problems. It is much better to correct the situation and wait for a year than to further compromise the lizard's well-being. This is especially true if a respiratory or other potentially communicable health problem exists with a potential breeder. Allowing a sick monitor to come in contact with a healthy mate is irresponsible.

Sexing

Monitors are among the more difficult lizards to accurately sex by utilizing external differences. The males of some species are larger and bulkier than the females and have proportion-

This white-throated monitor, V. albigularis, *is appropriately named. It does have a white throat. Some populations don't.*

ately larger heads. But these differences are proportional and often very subtle. A heavily gravid female may actually be considerably heavier than a similarly sized male. When near full term, an egg-laden female may show the lumpy outline of her eggs. Although sexual color differences are unusual among monitors, adult male Merten's water monitors often have the sides of their faces suffused with blue, whereas those of the females are orange-yellow. Males also have bulges at the base of the tail, and some male monitors have patches of modified scales at the tail base.

Of all sizes, the hatchlings of most species are the most easily sexed, and then only while they are a month or less in age. The hemipenes of hatchling males may be carefully and gently everted by utilizing the same "pressure and thumb-rolling" method breeders use to sex hatchling snakes. In this method the lizard is held upside down in one hand. The thumb of your other hand is placed subcaudally a few millimeters posterior to the lizard's vent, pressed firmly downward, and rolled gently forward (toward the vent). The pressure will cause the hemipenes of the male to evert. Females, of course, lack hemipenes, but will have a small reddish dot on the tissue on each side of the vent. Done improperly, this technique can injure your lizard. We strongly urge you to use the services of an experienced herpetoculturist until you are fully comfortable and adept with the procedure. "Probing," again similar to that done to sex snakes, can also be used. Probing, too, must be done very carefully (seek experienced help) and is not 100 percent accurate, even when done by experts.

There are times when, if you are observant, the lizard may inform you of its sex. Males, both young and old, may voluntarily evert or protrude their hemipenes if disturbed. They may do this occasionally while just foraging in their cage, but are most prone to resorting to hemipenial eversion if they are grasped, immobilized, and turned upside down. Be careful when doing this! The method often causes the frightened lizard to void its intestinal content as well. If hemipenial eversion does occur, you will, of course, be certain that the lizard is a male. But if it doesn't occur, you will not necessarily know for certain whether the specimen is a male that merely didn't choose to evert its hemipenis or a female that had none to evert.

Radiographing, occasionally done at zoos, can accurately sex monitors by showing the presence or lack of a pair of hemipenile bones, one on each side of and just posterior to the anal opening. Males have these bone spurs; females lack them. But radiography exposes the gonads to unnecessary radiation.

Let's Talk Temperature

What temperatures do we suggest for monitor husbandry? Let's look at a few examples. The following comments merely give some general ideas. Please check the various species accounts for additional comments. Note that the recommended temperatures for forest species of a given latitude vary less than those suggested for desert forms from the same latitude. This is simply because where tropical and subtropical temperatures are buffered by the forests, the day/night and season changes are usually noticeably less than in open deserts.

How long should the period of cooling be maintained? The truth is that in most cases no one really knows. Because so very little is known with certainty about the reproductive biology of most monitors, many of the suggestions contained in this section are extrapolations from what is known about better-understood lizards and snakes that dwell among the varanids.

With many of these other reptiles, the needed period of cooling varies from 30 to 75 days. It seems logical that a similar duration would be necessary for monitors, but experimentation is needed. Until known otherwise, we suggest that the winter regimen be maintained for a period of from 30 to 50 days.

Above all, keep records and disseminate knowledge. There are virtually no experts when it comes to monitor-breeding techniques, only some folks who have been more or less consistently luckier than others.

Does your monitor require a period of dormancy to cycle reproductively? Probably not. Would it hurt to provide your monitor with a period of dormancy? Again, probably not, especially if it is a species that normally encounters cool to cold winter temperatures in the wild. And a short period of dormancy might do some good.

Monitors from southern subtropical latitudes (southernmost Australia and Africa) undergo periodic dormancy. The times of quietude may be restricted to an occasional few days during the passage of a cold front or may be of longer duration in areas that are normally cool to cold. These lizards may also estivate for variable durations during periods of extreme heat or drought.

The problem, of course, is that once a monitor of any species enters the general pet trade, it is impossible to know from what latitude it originated. Occasionally specialty dealers can give you some idea of the origin of a specimen that they are offering, or, if the species in question comes from a circumscribed range, you can fairly well

Forest Species

	Summer Highs	Basking Spot		Winter Lows	Basking Spot
Day	84–88°F (29–31°C)	87–90°F (30–32°C)	Day	80–84°F (27–29°C)	84–88°F (29–31°C)
Night	76–80°F (24–27°C)	off	Night	68–72°F (20–22°C)	off

Desert Species

	Summer Highs	Basking Spot		Winter Lows	Basking Spot
Day	86–92°F (30–33°C)	90–98°F (32–37°C)	Day	72–76°F (22–24°C)	80–84°F (27–29°C)
Night	75–80°F (24–27°C)	off	Night	65–70°F (18–21°C)	off

narrow its origin and hence its climatic requirements. But if it's a widely ranging species such as the savanna or Nile monitor, the best you can ever do is guess. In most cases, the combination of parameters that we have suggested—the reduction of photoperiod, temperature, humidity, and feeding frequency—will probably be sufficient to stimulate reproductive cycling.

Whether your animals are maintained indoors or outdoors, learn to make the most of changes in barometric pressure. You will note that even those specimens kept indoors in cages where they are unable to see the outdoors become more active before and during a severe thunderstorm, the passage of a frontal system, or a tropical depression.

The activity of the lizards is caused by the lowering of the barometric pressure associated with such weather patterns. Use and enhance

HELPFUL HINT: As captives, teiids and monitors require much the same care, from spacious cages to health and stress controls.

these periods of naturally increased activity by misting, warming, cooling, adding a second male, or doing whatever else may enhance the possibility of sexual interest.

The male dominance factor (a male protecting his territory from incursions by another male) is known to be an important aspect of lizard behavior, especially in varanids and teiids. Inducing male dominance can be an important tool to the breeder of varanids, but it has to be carefully supervised by the keeper to avoid damage to the lizards. If worked to best advantage, it may sexually stimulate both males enough for both to repeatedly and successfully breed the females.

Breeding Your Tegus

It is not without justification that the macroteiids are often spoken of as the ecological equivalents of the monitors. Though teiids don't get as large as some of the monitors, teiids and monitors are of similar appearance, habits, and, for the most part, ecology.

Tegus are unusual in that they actually build

Hatching time for a clutch of red tegu eggs.

a nest suitable for egg deposition, another factor which you will need to consider and provide for.

Because there are so few species of tegus, the factors pertinent to the breeding of these teiid lizards (when known) are included in detail in the various species accounts. Those tegus bred with most success are the most southerly two, the black and white, *T. merianae*, and the red, *T. rufescens*. In both cases, the big lizards are being bred outdoors, and extrapolation from those conditions will be necessary if you wish to succeed in indoor facilities.

Nesting facilities: Both tegus and monitors bury their eggs, often deeply, in suitably warmed and moistened substrate. Large monitors dig nests about 30 inches (75 cm) in depth, and small species may dig nests only a few inches (to 10 cm) deep. In most cases, at least in captivity, the preferred medium seems to be earth, either brought into their indoor cages or

occurring naturally in outside facilities. In some cases deepened substrate has been provided in nesting boxes. Substrate that is too cold or too wet or too dry may induce the female monitor to retain eggs beyond their normal developmental duration. Ground surface temperatures of 85°F (29°C) to close to 100°F (37.7°C) have been reported at the nesting sites of various monitors.

The ground surface temperatures of many desert species are often understandably higher than those recorded for woodland/forest species. In all cases, at the time measured, the actual nest temperature was considerably cooler—76°F (24°C) to about 82°F (28°C).

In all cases of captive breeding, the eggs were removed from the nests and incubated artificially. As mentioned, success has varied, and additional knowledge and experimentation is needed from both the professional and amateur herpetoculturists who choose to work with these magnificent lizards.

INTRODUCTION TO THE MONITORS

Within the ranks of the monitors are the world's largest as well as some comparatively tiny lizard species. It is an unwieldy family, within which several subgenera have been established in an effort to recognize the differences between the members of that genus.

The Lizard Family Varanidae

All monitors are protected by international conservation treaties, and many by specific laws of the various countries to which they are indigenous.

Monitors may be found in Asia, Africa, Australia, and Indonesia. These intriguing and very predaceous lizards vary in size from the heavy-bodied 10 feet (3 m) attained by males of the Indonesian Komodo monitor, *Varanus komodoensis* (also called "dragon lizard"), down to the barely 8-inch (20-cm) overall length of the Australian short-tailed monitor, *V. brevicauda*. Between these extremes are some 40 to 50 additional species of more moderate lengths.

Monitors are thought to be the most snake-like of the lizards. They have greatly protrusible

The Komodo dragon is the bulkiest of the monitors.

tongues and well-developed Jacobson's organs on the roof of the mouth to analyze the chemosensory data brought in by the tongue. All monitors have well-developed eyelids and easily discernible ear openings.

All have a more or less attenuate form (with the African savanna and white-throated monitors proportionately the heaviest at all stages of their lives and the adults of the Komodo dragon especially robust).

All have strong, well-developed legs with five toes on each foot.

The claws can be recurved and needle sharp to assist with climbing, sharp but less recurved (rock-dwelling species), or considerably blunter and of little use in climbing (certain terrestrial forms).

Monitors' tails lack fracture planes and are nonregenerable.

All monitors are oviparous.

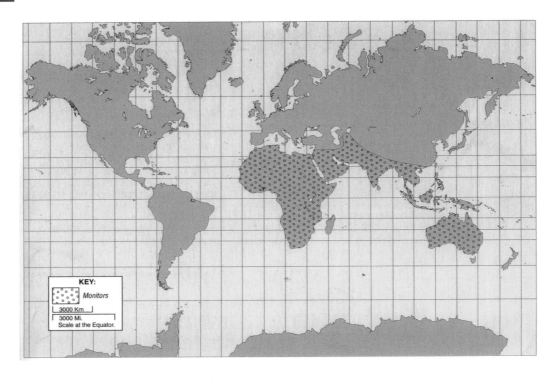

KEY:

Monitors

3000 Km.
3000 Mi.
Scale at the Equator.

Although monitors are not capable of any great degree of color change, cool specimens are often somewhat darker than warm ones. The darker hues facilitate rapid warming (thermoregulation), whereas the lighter shades reflect heat, thus helping to prevent a critical overwarming.

Monitors are all highly predatory, consuming, according to their sizes and abilities, insects, fish, amphibians, other reptiles, eggs, rodents, birds, hares, and in the case of the gigantic

Monitor climbing, showing attenuate form, protrusible tongue, eyelids, ear opening, strong legs and claws.

Precise on young mangrove monitors, V. indicus (above), the markings are more obscure on adults (below).

seen sporadically. Only two are in the low-to-moderate price range. These are the African savanna monitor and the African Nile monitor. Other more expensive species that are occasionally seen are the white-throated monitor, of African origin, the Asian water monitor, the mangrove monitor of the Moluccan Islands (including the beautiful blue-tailed morph) and two Indonesian tree monitors, the green and the black. Of the smaller semiarboreal species, the Timor is often available, and of the terrestrial/saxicolous monitors, the Australian ridge-tailed is now the most frequently offered.

Komodo monitor, goats, deer, and similarly sized animals.

Nine monitor species regularly are available to the pet trade, and at least three more are

HELPFUL HINT: For monitors, food items do not need to be alive, or even fresh.

SOME PET STORE FAVORITES

Monitors in the pet marketplace are wild-caught rather than captive born.

African Monitors

Of the three most commonly seen African monitors, two are stocky landlubbers that attain a length of about 5 feet (1.5 m), and the other is a more attenuated semiaquatic species that occasionally exceeds 7 feet (2 m) in length. The first two, the savanna and the white-throated monitors, were long thought to be conspecific. Although quite similar externally and closely related, the savanna and the white-throated monitors are sufficiently dissimilar to warrant their current taxonomic separation into two species. In older texts you will find white-throated monitors listed as a subspecies of the savanna.

It should also be noted that in some of its populations the common name of "white-throated monitor" applied to *Varanus*

A beautiful baby of the black-throated morph of the white-throated monitor.

albigularisis is clearly erroneous. Many specimens have off-white, dusky, or even black throats.

Savanna and white-throated monitors display a remarkable tolerance (immunity?) to the venom of many of the snake species that live in the same habitat.

The Savanna Monitor
Varanus exanthematicus

The African savanna monitor, *V. exanthematicus*, is immensely popular in the pet trade. It is a grayish species with darker and lighter markings and much enlarged, roughened nuchal (nape) scales. The dorsal markings of juveniles often take the form of crossbands of light-centered dark eyelike ocelli. The body color is lighter and prettier when the lizard is warm and unstressed.

The savanna monitor is a proportionately stocky, dry-land species. It commonly attains a length of about 5 feet (1.5 m), and some

An adult of the black-throated morph of the white-throated monitor.

specimens may near 6 feet (2 m). With advanced age, during times of plenty, savanna monitors can become grossly obese. It is probably no more healthy for a monitor to be decidedly overweight than it is for a human. Reasonable efforts should be made to keep the weight of captive savanna monitors within acceptable parameters. Unfortunately, no monitor size/weight chart has yet been produced. Your intuition will necessarily be your guide, but be aware—fat is not better, especially if you are hoping for longevity records or breeding success.

Frightened specimens huff and puff and inflate their bodies and gular areas alarmingly, turn sideways to the perceived threat, and lash with their tails. Tame specimens forgo this and will often actually crawl onto their owners' laps. As this indicates, savanna monitors can become very tame. However, they are also always ready to eat. They quickly learn to associate the presence of a human with food. Be careful when initially reaching for them. A bite by a large specimen, intended or not, can be a painful ordeal!

Savanna, white-throated, and some other monitor species use an interesting ploy when confronted by a large predator. When severely frightened, the lizards arc their bodies and grasp a hind limb in the mouth. In this position they present a larger, and perhaps unappealing aspect, to the confronting predator. Similar defensive positioning is used by other distinctly different lizards, the armadillo lizard, *Cordylus cataphractus*, being the best known.

About breeding: Although monitors of many kinds are considered difficult to breed, both private hobbyists and zoological gardens have succeeded a few times with the savanna monitor. Because of the vast number of wild-collected babies being imported for the pet trade, the prices of savanna monitors are so deflated that no large-scale captive-breeding programs have been instituted. Thus only the most dedicated of hobbyists, those who wish to breed savanna monitors for research rather than monetary gain, have bred the species. It is encouraging that at

The Monitors of Africa
Subgenus *Polydaedalus*

Varanus a. albigularis, South African white-throated monitor, Southern Africa
V. albigularis angolensis, Angolan white-throated monitor, Angola
V. albigularis microstictus, East African white-throated monitor, Kenya and Tanzania
V. niloticus, Nile monitor, sub-Saharan Africa
V. ornatus, ornate monitor, tropical west Africa
V. yemensis, Yemen monitor, Yemen

Savanna or Savannah? It's all in the preference and the country! In the United
States, a savanna(h) is defined as a treeless
plain. Savannah is also a major city in the
state of Georgia. We prefer to delete the
final "h" when speaking of a geologic phe-
nomenon and to use the "h" when speaking
of the Georgia city.

least some are seriously working with this monitor. Although it is still rather common over much
of its sub-Sarahan range, no species can perpetually withstand the onslaught of the pet and
skin trades. Someday the importations of this
species will come to a screeching halt (as they
have for other once commonly seen species), and
we will then be dependent on the knowledge
gained from those who chose to learn before it
was actually necessary to do so. Then their wisdom may begin to benefit them financially.

Male monitors are not only territorial, but
extremely defensive of their territories. This is
especially true during the breeding season.
Although they may wander widely, keen vision
and an equally keen olfactory sense reliably
inform monitors of interlopers. During the
breeding season interlopers are quickly investi-
gated, with males being challenged, females
being bred, and juveniles being ignored (if large
but yet subadult) or eaten. Readers of natural
history books or watchers of nature channels on
TV may well be familiar with the territorial and
breeding-related grapplings of the male monitors. Each male raises its torso high from the
ground, and while in a tripedal stance (supported
by hind limbs and tail) grapples and rakes at the
other with its foreclaws in an attempt to topple
and dominate the opponent. In some instances,
rear claws are employed as well. These interac-

tions may be important to successful breedings
by many monitor species, the savanna among
them; the drama may be nearly as important in
captivity as in the wild.

In nature, it is usually the dominant male that
"wins" the female. Dominance and territoriality
certainly seem to figure prominently in the
reproductive readiness of varanid lizards.

Clutches of as many as 50 eggs have been
recorded, but most clutches are half that size
or fewer. A chamber dug into the side of a
termitarium may occasionally be used, but
apparently over much of its range the female
savanna monitor merely digs a hole in moist,
easily worked earth.

The White-Throated Monitor
V. albigularis ssp.

Like the savanna monitor, the white-throated
monitor is a very heavy-bodied, terrestrial species.
Some become tame if acquired when young and
worked with diligently, but most seem more difficult to tame than savanna monitors. In fact, even
with considerable attention, many white-throated
monitors remain quite irascible.

Handling an unruly adult can be a painful
proposition. It can be difficult, especially for a
new enthusiast, to differentiate between some
specimens of the white-throated and the
savanna monitors. In general, white-throated
monitors are darker and more strongly banded
than savannas. On the white-throated, the top
of the head and the nape, between the nearly
black temporal stripes (which may be well
defined or obscure and either converge or
diverge on the posterior nape) are usually especially dark. The tail is prominently banded.

Although both hobbyists and herpetoculturists
had long referred to *V. albigularis* as a separate

White-throated monitors are the third most popular African species.

species, it was only in 1989 that the savanna and white-throated monitors were officially (scientifically) separated. Long-overdue research dictated the change. In that year, the official name of the newly elevated species became *Varanus albigularis*, and the species was then quickly separated into a number of questionable subspecies. Besides the nominate form, there are *V. a. microstictus* (questionably valid) and *V. a. ionidesi* (now invalid, although pet dealers still use the designation).

In 1989, a new species, *V. yemenesis*, was described. Since then its validity has been questioned by some taxonomists and accepted by others. The value of characteristics used to separate this big lizard from *V. albigularis*, its closest relative, will probably be bandied around for years. Only time will tell whether the scientific community will accept the Yemen monitor as a fully distinct species.

The babies of the white-throated monitor are strikingly marked. Hatchlings have a dark head that, with growth, becomes progressively darker. The dark temporal and nuchal stripes are particularly well developed on the young. These may be retained by adults, but the progressive suffusing of the head and shoulders with dark pigment often obliterates the markings.

Attaining somewhat more than 6 feet (2 m), Tanzanian white-throats (with black throats!) were once considered the subspecies *V. a. ionidesi*. They were popularly referred to as Ionides' monitors, after the animal hunter/dealer. Although the subspecific status is no longer recognized, these do seem to be distinctively patterned and colored lizards.

White-throated monitors have been bred in captivity. At 84°F (29°C) the eggs hatch in about 150 days. Typical clutches contain 6 to 25 eggs.

In the wild, clutches of up to 37 eggs have been found. Deposition sites vary. Some females seem to prefer digging their nests into the almost concrete-hard termitaria that dot their habitats. In an effort to retain the humidity so necessary to their existence, the insects soon reconstruct the mound, thus protecting the monitor eggs now contained within. In other cases, the nest is merely dug in moisture-retaining damp earth. When subjected to the vagaries of natural incubation, it may take the eggs in some nests nearly a year to hatch.

Although the two are now considered separate species, most of what has been said about the savanna monitor applies equally to the white-throat.

The Nile Monitors
V. niloticus and *V. ornatus*

There are two species of big, yellow spotted monitors in Africa. The Nile monitor, *V. niloticus*, is a veldt and savanna species, whereas the ornate monitor (sometimes referred to as the ornate Nile monitor or the forest monitor), *V. ornatus,* is largely restricted to the tropical west African forests.

Despite a typically bad disposition (which may or may not become more gentle with handling), these pretty and relatively inexpensive monitors are common pet trade species, both in Europe and America.

As babies, whether resting quietly on a limb, peering quizzically from a hide box, or moving slowly and methodically through the cage, either Nile monitor is an attractive and engaging little creature. However, most Nile monitors do not tame sufficiently to make particularly good pets (a fact that vendors often fail to mention).

Despite their ready availability, we don't rec- ommend these species to any but the most dedicated and experienced of hobbyists. If larger than hatchlings when collected, there is probably no species of monitors harder to tame.

Both kinds of Nile monitors are darker in color when young than when adult. Both have cross-bands of yellow spots.

Compared to the ornate monitor (bottom), the Nile monitor has a busy and less well-defined pattern (top).

Once a subspecies of the Nile monitor, the ornate monitor, *V. ornatus*, is now afforded full species status. It is a particularly pretty monitor. From shoulder to pelvic girdle, this species has four to five rows (rarely six) of large rounded, dark-outlined yellow spots. These contrast strongly with the buffered black of the rest of the body. The yellow spots lengthen into short crossbars posteriorly and are complete bands on the tail.

Varanus niloticus is more variable than *V. ornatus* and usually has more than six rows of yellow spots. The body color may vary from solid black to black well buffered (lightened) with the tiniest of yellowish pepperings on hatchlings to olive brown on adults. Its limbs are usually well marked with prominent discrete spots, but may be finely peppered with yellow in some phases. From one to four U-shaped yellow markings are usually present on the rear of the head and the nape.

When walking, both the Nile and ornate monitor holds its body well above the substrate on powerful legs, while the long motile tongue busily probes every nook and cranny, searching for prey or an avenue of escape, should the latter become necessary.

The Nile monitor is the more commonly seen of these two species in captivity, but suggestions for captive care pertain to the ornate monitor as well. If frightened or engaged in territorial behavior, Nile monitors indulge in typical impressive and effective defense and threat postures. The body is inflated with air, but compressed vertically. The monitor stands high on its legs, hisses, whips the tail (which, by the way, is a very effective, attention-getting defense), and bites if the opportunity occurs.

In the wild, female Nile monitors show a decided preference for nesting in the termitaria

HELPFUL HINT: If fed adequately and kept suitably warm, hatchlings will grow quickly.

that are found in their habitats. Within the termite mound, the termites maintain a steady temperature and high humidity. That the female monitors are able to dig through the mounds' sunbaked outer shell—barricades legendarily of almost concretelike hardness—is mute testimony to the effectiveness of the sharp claws and the strength of the lizards' legs.

In some cases it may take the female monitor several days to complete the nest. After egg deposition has been completed, the termites repair their mound. The closure again retains temperatures and humidity ideal for the development of the monitor eggs.

In captivity, female Nile monitors dig a deep nesting chamber in moist (not wet) earth. They may more readily do so if the earth is contained in a barrel or is secluded behind some sort of opaque barrier. The female will have to be comfortable and unstressed to nest. Unless conditions are conducive to nesting, the female Nile monitor may just scatter her eggs on the floor of her cage or, worse yet, retain them until egg solidification or adherence occurs, which require surgical intervention.

Nile monitors lay large clutches. More than 15 eggs are normally laid, and clutches of more than 50 have been recorded.

In nature, the eggs may take the better part of a year to incubate, the hatchlings emerging from their termite mound cavity when the summer rains soften the exterior somewhat. Incubation in captivity may take somewhat less than half that expected in the wild.

There may be no monitor species more strikingly colored than a hatchling Dumeril's monitor, V. dumerilii.

A sizable water container—one large enough for the lizard to climb in and submerge—should be provided for this species.

Although most adults are smaller, Nile monitors can attain a length of more than 6.5 feet (2 m). The babies, which are quite arboreal, are opportunistic feeders on insects and other arthropods, carrion, smaller lizards, nestling rodents, or whatever else they can ferret out. They use both visual and chemical cues when hunting. Their long snouts serve them in good stead, allowing them to grasp insects in narrow spaces.

With growth, many changes occur in the Nile monitor. The skull becomes heavier and the snout less attenuate. This allows the lizard to easily overpower the mollusk, crustacean, fish, and mammalian components of its diet. The Nile monitor's fondness for crocodile eggs is well documented and often mentioned. With increased size, the Nile monitor becomes less arboreal, returning instead to terrestrial and aquatic habitats. It is a powerful swimmer that may be seen some distance from land.

Note: As a result of released unwanted pets, the Nile monitor is now established in Cape Coral and has been seen in other regions of Florida. Sightings first occurred in 1990, but no evidence of breeding was found. This large and very predatory lizard is now firmly established in the state. Despite eradication programs, both adults and hatchlings continue to be seen. The Cape Coral population is of considerable concern to conservationists who believe that the big lizards may prey on the burrowing owl population.

Asian/Indonesian Monitors

The Asian and Indonesian monitors are no longer considered inexpensive. Even the once commonly imported Asian water monitor, *V. salvator* ssp., commands prices of more than $100. Nor are any of the Asian monitors as readily available in the pet trade as the three African species already discussed.

Dumeril's Monitor and Rough-Necked Monitor
V. dumerilii ssp. and *V. rudicollis*

The Malaysian Dumeril's monitor, *V. dumerilii* ssp., is spectacular as a hatchling and reasonably attractive as a good-sized adult. Hatchlings have fire-orange heads and yellow crossbars on a black body. With growth the head color and yellow of the bands all too quickly fade to olive tan or olive gray and the black lightens to olive brown. Once acclimated, Dumeril's monitors are quiet and easily cared for. They attain a length of somewhat more than 5 feet (1.5 m) and are sporadically available in the pet trades of both America and Europe. The nuchal (nape) scales of most specimens seen in the pet trade are promi-

Long before it is one third grown, the orange head of the Dumeril's monitor has faded to brown.

nently enlarged but flattened, producing a tiled, rather than a roughened, tuberculate effect. The large scales continue down the lizard's back. The nuchal scales of Borneo specimens (seldom seen in the pet trade) tend to be more keeled. The dorsal scales of the Bornean Dumeril's monitor are smaller than the nuchal scales.

Dumeril's Monitor and Relatives
Subgenus *Empagusia*

Varanus bengalensis, Bengal monitor, India, Pakistan, Bangladesh, Iran, Sri Lanka, Thailand, southern China, Myanmar

Varanus dumerilii, Dumeril's monitor, Thailand, Myanmar, Malay Penninsula, Borneo, and Sumatra

Varanus flavescens, Indian yellow monitor, India, Pakistan, Bangladesh

Varanus nebulosus, clouded monitor, Java to Thailand

Varanus rudicollis, rough-necked monitor, Thailand, Myanmar, Sumatra, Malay Peninsula, Borneo

Adults of Dumeril's monitor are often mistaken for the rough-necked monitor, *V. rudicollis*, a species of similar size but very dissimilar appearance, that often is imported in the same shipments.

As a juvenile the rough-necked monitor lacks the orange head and yellow bars, having instead very thin, light gray crossbars on a ground color of deep brown. The rough-necked monitor also has a very slender head and a particularly slender snout. The snout of the Dumeril's monitor is broad and rather flat— typically monitorlike. The larger, prominently projecting nape scales of *V. rudicollis* are also distinguishing characteristics. When the rough-necked monitor is viewed in profile, the individual points of the nape scale keels are readily seen.

The rough-necked monitor is a persistently arboreal species; Dumeril's is considerably less so, at least as an adult.

Like most other monitors, the vast majority of *V. dumerilii* in the pet trade of the world are wild-collected specimens.

Although extensively arboreal, the rough-necked monitor, V. rudicollis, often descends to the ground.

Captive breedings have occasionally been reported. Clutches of 4 to as many as 18 eggs have been mentioned. Because so little captive breeding has been done, the optimum egg incubation temperature remains unknown. Temperatures as low as 82°F (28°C) have apparently produced successful incubations. Certainly, a newly hatched clutch of babies of this species must be one of the most spectacular sights known to monitor keepers. In the wild, Dumeril's monitors seem most abundant in littoral, estuarine, and riverine habitats. Adults are far more apt to take to the water than to the trees when startled. In keeping with this habit, captives should be provided with a water receptacle large enough for the lizard to clamber into, coil, and submerge. Because many monitors defecate in water, it will be necessary to clean and sterilize the water container at frequent intervals. Be certain that whatever receptacle you provide is easily handled.

Initially nervous, especially if a larger size when trapped, a Dumeril's monitor will usually quiet down rather rapidly once given secure caging and a suitable hiding area. Seldom do specimens bite as frenziedly as other monitor species when restrained. They will, however, posture, hiss, and slap with their tails. Specimens that feel particularly threatened become semirigid and point their noses skyward, often closing their eyes as they do so. This posture is usually assumed by the subordinate specimen, either in the presence of a predator or in appeasement of another monitor.

Crustaceans, mollusks, nestling birds, and small mammals seem to figure prominently in the diet of larger specimens. Insects, fish, and some carrion are also eaten, especially by smaller specimens.

Adult rough-necked monitors may exceed 4.5 feet (1.4 m) in total length. The fact that they are a slender, long-necked, long-legged lizard with an attenuated, semiprehensile tail (about 60–65 percent of the overall length) causes them to look smaller than they actually are.

When startled, the rough-necked monitor usually tries to go upward. A vertically oriented cage will best serve its needs. A nervous monitor, a

Note the slender bird-like snout and head of the hatchling rough-necked monitor.

rough-neck will readily use elevated hide boxes, and seems especially at home when tangles of branches and other such visual barriers are provided. It becomes even more secure when real or artificial vining plants are draped over the cage-top branches.

Like most monitors, *V. rudicollis* has been bred in captivity, but only infrequently, and more often by European than by American hobbyists. Suggested incubation temperature for the 4 to 14 eggs is 82–84°F (28–29°C). At these temperatures, incubation takes about six months.

Although rough-necked monitors may not use a large soaking bowl as frequently as many other monitor species, they nonetheless enjoy a long soak occasionally.

Freshly imported specimens of both the Dumeril's and rough-necked monitors can prove to be reluctant feeders. Dumeril's can usually be coaxed into accepting standard monitor fare—insects, small mice, high-quality canned reptile or cat foods, even some suitably sized fish. On the other hand, *V. rudicollis* can be a problematic holdout. Insects, small tree frogs,

small lizards, and (occasionally) newborn mice might tempt them. We have had to force-feed some particularly debilitated specimens to get them started. We consider the rough-necked monitor a rather delicate and problematic captive.

The Tree Monitors: Emerald, Black, Yellow, and Blue

The emerald tree monitor and the black tree monitor, *V. prasinus* and *V. beccarii*, have long been popular with monitor enthusiasts. Both are so slender that they may appear emaciated, and both have strongly prehensile tails. The yellow and the blue tree monitors, *V. melinus* and *V. macraei*, are relatively new in the pet trade and somewhat larger. They also are proportionately heavier, and have only moderately prehensile tails.

The names of all are descriptive. The emerald tree monitor is just that, a beautiful leaf green with black highlights. The black tree monitor is clad in scales of ebony. The yellow and the blue tree monitors are grayish but bear a suffusion of either yellow or blue.

Tree Monitors and Relatives

Grouped in the subgenus *Euprepiosaurus*

Varanus beccarii, black tree monitor, Aru Islands, New Guinea

V. boehmei, Waigeo Tree monitor, Waigeo Island, Solomon Islands

V. bogerti, Louisiade emerald tree monitor, Louisiade Archipelago, New Guinea

V. caeruliverens, Halmahera blue-spotted monitor, Halmahera, Island, Solomon Islands

V. cerambonensis, Ambon mangrove monitor, Moluccan Islands

V. doreanus, New Guinea blue-tailed monitor, New Guinea, northern Cape York Peninsula, Australia, and nearby islands

V. finschi, Finsch's monitor, Bismarck Archipelago

V. indicus, Mangrove monitor, Indo-Pacific coastal areas

V. jobiensis, peach-throated monitor, New Guinea

V. juxindicus, Rennell Island mangrove monitor, Rennel Island, Solomon Islands

V. keithhornei, Cape York emerald monitor, Cape York Peninsula, Australia

V. kordensis, Kordo emerald tree monitor, Kordo region, New Guinea (questionable validity)

V. maccraei, blue tree monitor, Batanta, Irian Jaya

V. melinus, yellow tree monitor, Obi, Moluccan Islands

V. prasinus, emerald monitor, New Guinea, nearby islands in the Torres Straits

V. reisingeri, Misol Island emerald tree monitor, Misol Island, New Guinea

V. spinulosus, Solomon Islands keeled monitor, Georges Island, Solomon Islands

V. telenesetes, Rossel Island black tree monitor, Rossel Island

V. yuwonoi, Tri-colored monitor, Halmahera Island, Solomon Islands

V. zugorum, Silver mangrove monitor, Halmahera Island, Solomon Islands

Emerald Monitors and Black Monitors

V. prasinus and *V. beccarii*

Note: As you will see from the list above, there are now many species of emerald and black monitors. Most look almost identical, having been separated by range and molecular data (DNA). In most cases it will prove futile (or at least very expensive) to ascertain an exact species. *Prasinus* and *beccarii* are the species most commonly seen in captivity.

Although both are long, lithe, and prehensile-tailed, the emerald and the black monitors are easily differentiated by color. The former has a leaf-green dorsum (occasionally considerably duller) across which usually run bands or spots of jet black (occasionally almost entirely lacking). The aptly named black tree monitor is entirely black in coloration.

Neither exceeds 34 inches (85 cm), of which somewhat more than 60 percent is slender, prehensile tail length. The tail is prehensile enough to support the monitor's entire body weight if necessary. The tail is usually loosely coiled when the monitor is at rest and wrapped loosely around a support when the lizard is active. The limbs are long and powerful, and the toes are tipped with sharp, recurved claws.

Adult emerald tree monitors (above) are less vividly marked than the juveniles.

Tree monitors' long, sharp teeth and extremely powerful jaws are designed to quickly overpower the lizards, frogs, small mammals, and birds on which these species prey. We hasten to assure you that they are most effective on restraining fingers and hands as well.

The New Guinean emerald tree monitor, *V. prasinus*, is a species of the lower elevations of New Guinea and some of the surrounding islands. Although emerald monitors seem less common far inland than in suitable habitats along the periphery of the island, this may be more a result of collectors' sampling techniques than of actuality. Certainly it is easier to collect along the coast than it is to penetrate deeply into the forests.

Emeralds are one of the prettiest of all monitors, coveted by private collectors and zoos alike. They usually prove quite hardy and soon accept small mice as prey. However, a variety of prey is thought to be better for the lizards in the long run than mice alone. Crickets, grasshoppers, June

beetles (easily collected around porch lights in the spring), king mealworms, and mice seem to be the most readily available. Some tree monitors will also accept an occasional strip of lean beef, good-quality canned cat food, and Monitor Diet. Large slugs were especially relished by some tree monitors that we maintained. After eating one of these slimy creatures, the monitors would laboriously wipe the sides of their mouths against branches and leaves to remove the slug's viscid mucus.

A daytime thermal gradient of about 84–92°F (28.8–33°C) with a relative humidity of 75 percent or more is satisfactory. Nighttime temperatures can be a few degrees cooler—68–75°F (20–24°C) is a good range—and no "hot spot" or thermal gradient is necessary.

Because of their arboreal tendencies, emerald monitors should be housed in a tall cage and provided with a number of limbs large enough for climbing. Secretive species, they will fully use the hiding places provided by growing plants, securely affixed hollow limbs, or even cockatiel nesting boxes.

When their cage habitat is being built, provide elevated basking limbs, accessed by diagonally affixed tree trunks. Some keepers prefer flat plywood shelves to limbs, but we have found the plywood more difficult to keep clean and odorless. It is a good idea (although probably not mandatory) to provide an individual basking perch at about the same level for every emerald in a cage. This often provides a degree of harmony not possible if the dominant specimen restricts subordinate specimens' access to a single desirable basking limb. A basking "hot spot"— 95–98°F (35–36.6°C)—should be provided on each perch. When multiple bulbs are used to provide several warmed basking areas, care must be taken not to overheat the cage.

Although reproductive success with this remarkable monitor remains the exception rather than the rule, the emerald monitor has been bred by several zoos and by private hobbyists as well. More success has been experienced in Europe than in the United States. The reported clutches are small, numbering from as few as two eggs to five eggs.

At 86°F (30°C), the incubation takes slightly less than five months, and hatchlings vary from a reported 3.5 inches (9 cm) to well over 5 inches (13 cm) in total length. If proper care is given, the growth of this monitor is rapid. A subadult size can be attained within the first year. The age at which sexual maturity is reached is still unknown, but it is probably not until two or even three years.

As is the case with many slender-bodied forest reptiles from habitats of high humidity, imported emerald and black tree monitors are often seriously dehydrated and stressed by the rigors of collection, holding, and shipping. It is imperative that a program of rehydration be begun immediately upon arrival (these species will usually respond well to a hydration chamber, pages 28 to 29). Stool samples or a cloacal wash should be taken and analyzed and an effective parasiticide given, if necessary.

The long and lanky black tree monitor, V. beccarii, is perfectly adapted for an arboreal life.

A portrait of a black tree monitor.

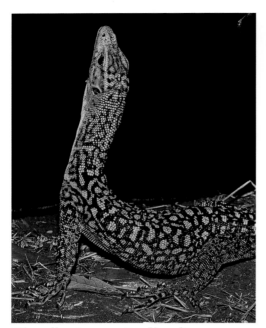

The yellow tree monitor, V. melinus, is a beautiful newcomer in the American pet market.

Nearly everything said about the emerald tree monitor applies equally to the black tree monitor. Even less is known about the reproductive biology of this species than is known about its green cousin. Clutch size seems the same, and preferred incubation temperatures are probably identical. This species has been bred in Europe, but we are unaware of successes by American hobbyists.

V. beccarii is another accomplished arborealist with a fully prehensile tail that is more than twice the SVL (snout–vent length). Often kept in a watchspring coil when the lizard is resting, the tail is usually held against a branch or loosely entwines it when the lizard is active.

Like the emerald monitors, *V. beccarii* often become severely dehydrated during importation procedures. A program of rehydration (see the section on hydration chambers, pages 28 to 29) should be immediately instituted. Once satisfactorily rehydrated, providing warmth—daytimes, 84–92°F (29–33°C) with a basking hot spot nearing 98°F (37°C)—and high cage humidity will do much to ensure successful acclimatization. During acclimatization, overall nighttime cage temperatures should be allowed to drop only slightly. After complete stabilization, nighttime temperatures can be allowed to fall into the high 60s or low 70sF (19–23°C). At all times, both during and after stabilization, a feeling of seclusion and security, as well as high cage humidity, must be provided for black tree monitors.

The shy and active black tree monitors do best if provided with large, vertically oriented cages. They will readily and habitually use firmly affixed hollow limbs, cockatiel nest boxes with easy access, or tangles of crisscrossed branches placed well above floor level, and especially near the top of the cage.

If grasped carelessly, black tree monitors defend themselves by biting, scratching, and voiding their cloacal contents. The teeth are long and very sharp, and the lizards do not readily release their grip. The long legs and toes are powerful, and the claws are of needlelike sharpness. You will probably wish to release your hold on the lizard long before it chooses to release its hold on you!

The Mangrove Monitor

V. indicus

Once quite uncommon in the pet industry, mangrove monitors are now seen with some regularity in specialty shops and on reptile dealers' lists. Although even now far from inexpensive, these pretty, moderately sized monitors are available to hobbyists who are able to afford them. *V. indicus* occurs along coastal North Australia and over most of the rest of the range of the species. Many of the specimens that enter the American pet trade are imported from the Solomon Islands.

In coloration *V. indicusis* has a black (occasionally olive or olive-brown) ground color liberally peppered with small discrete yellow, cream, greenish, or white spots. The light spots are usually arranged in cross rows dorsally, but are more variably arranged laterally, where they are often more numerous. Thus, the lateral surfaces may appear somewhat lighter in color than the dorsum. Hatchlings and juveniles are more brilliantly colored than adults, and some juveniles may bear secondary rows of pale blue spots between the yellow. The tail of juveniles is often vividly banded in black and white. Mangrove monitors may occasionally exceed 5 feet (1.5 m) in total length, but of this, most is tail.

If acquired young and handled often and gently, mangrove monitors tame fairly well. Large wild-collected specimens have formidable jaw

Profile of a yellow-spotted blue-tailed monitor, V. caeruliverens.

TIP

A Watering Tip

Arboreal monitors (like many other arboreally oriented lizards) may not readily descend to the ground to drink from a pan. This is especially true of disoriented, newly imported lizards that, until capture, probably derived most (if not all) of their water requirements from water-filled tree holes and from lapping water flowing down limbs, trunks, and foliage during storms. For these lizards it is best to place a water receptacle on an elevated shelf near a favored basking or resting area. We have found that both the emerald and black tree monitors will readily drink from an elevated water dish, placed in the pot of an easily accessible hanging plant. They seem to notice, and be drawn to, the plant by the fresh droplets of water that remain on the leaves after mistings. It is very important that you place all water dishes where they are conspicuous.

The blue-tailed monitor, **V. doreanus,** *is a beautiful species of moderate size.*

power and sharp claws and can be a real chore to handle.

Even large specimens may become more gentle with time and handling. Mangrove monitors have mastered several media. They are admirable climbers, entirely at home in the water, and comfortable on land. However, if hard-pressed, they will usually take to the water if it is present, thus indicating their aquatic preferences. These monitors are often encountered in trees along fresh water billabongs but may be particularly common in mangrove-studded brackish and saltwater locations. This species has a wide range over much of southern Asia and northern Australia.

In keeping with their aquatic propensities, mangrove monitors feed on numerous creatures of their riparian and littoral habitats. Small specimens are adept at catching worms, snails, fish, crayfish, and the like. Some amount of carrion is also eaten, and if nestling, rodents or birds of suitable size are probably eaten.

Larger specimens have been reported feeding on all of the above, as well as small turtles,

snakes, and lizards. Captives will also accept lean raw meat. Robert Sprackland, who has kept this species for many years, has commented that the lizards seem to have problems digesting large mammalian prey. He suggests that mice, rather than rats, be offered to even large mangrove monitors.

As captives, mangrove monitors require spacious cages, hide boxes, firmly affixed, elevated perches, and a sizable but easily cleaned water pan. Captives will spend hours (sometimes days) coiled in their water receptacles. They may remain submerged between breaths for the better part of an hour. This is a warmth-loving monitor that seems to thrive at a cage temperature of 85–92°F (29–33°C). A basking area with a temperature of 96°F (35.5°C) will be used to thermoregulate, especially if the remainder of the cage is kept in the mid-80sF (29°C).

Like most other wild-collected monitors, fresh imports of the mangrove monitor can bear heavy loads of endoparasites. These should be identified and purged if the lizard's health seems to be affected.

Blue-tailed monitors are rather like a color enhanced mangrove monitor in appearance.

Comments on the Blue-Tailed and the Peach-Throated Monitors

Both blue-tailed and peach-throated monitors have traditionally been sold by dealers as variants of the mangrove monitor or whatever names the dealer thinks will sell.

The blue-tailed monitor may be offered in the pet trade by the erroneous scientific name of *V. kalibecki*. The correct scientific name is *Varanus doreanus*.

The body color of the blue-tailed monitor is very similar to that of the mangrove monitor. However, the yellow dorsal dots of the blue-tailed monitor are larger. As indicated by its common name, the tail of this lizard is banded in black and blue (rather than in black and white). It is a very beautiful lizard that is much in demand as a baby by the pet industry. It attains only about 3.5 to 4 feet (2.7–3 m) in total length. The specimens in the pet trade of the world are probably collected in western Irian Jaya.

The true identity of the peach-throated monitor is equally problematic. This lizard was described in 1932 as a race of the mangrove monitor. Then called *Varanus indicus jobiensis*, it has since been referred to in error as *V. karlschmidti*. Its correct scientific name is *V. jobiensis*.

The peach-throated monitor is a pretty but quietly colored lizard. It does have a peach or orange throat, may have the vaguest blush of deepest blue on the distal portion of the tail, and is otherwise black, marked with the tiniest of yellow dots. The dots often coalesce into vague bands both dorsally and laterally. The head often lacks yellow speckling. The head conformation of this lizard seems more angular than on nominate *V. indicus*.

The natural history of this uncommon New Guinean monitor remains enigmatic.

We can find no reports of either the blue-tailed or the peach-throated monitors having been bred in captivity. Care for both should be similar to that provided the mangrove monitor.

The Asian Water Monitors

At one time the Asian water monitor was thought to be just a single species, *V. salvator*, with a huge range and a variable appearance.

The Species of Water Monitors
Subgenus *Soterosaurus*

Varanus andamanensis, Andaman Islands
water monitor, Andaman Islands
V. cumingi, Cumings (Philippine golden)
water monitor, Mindanao, Samar, Layte,
Bohol, Basilan, Philippines
V. marmoratus, marbled water monitor,
Luzon, Samer, Ticas, Palawan, Calamia,
Sogon, Mindoro, and Sulu Islands
V. nuchalis, Negros (white-headed) water
monitor, Negros, Cebu, Tacas, Panay, and
Masbate, Philippines
V. s. salvator, Common (Asian) water moni-
tor, India to Sri Lanka and Thailand to
Irian Jaya
V. salvator bivittatus, Javan two-striped
water monitor, Java
V. species, black water monitor, Malaya
Peninsula highlands
V. togianus, Togian water monitor, Sulawesi
and surrounding islands

When it became apparent that the variations were consistent within a certain population, sub-species were described. A few years later genetic differences (usually mitochondrial DNA [mtDNA]) were added to the equation, and various sub-species were elevated to full species status and previously undescribed species were differentiated.

As of mid-2006, rather than one wide-ranging, difficult-to-define water monitor, the former Asian water monitor is a species complex of six easily identified species, each having a rather well-defined range. One more species, a big black monster from the Malayan highlands, awaits description.

Not all of these monitors are readily available in the pet trade. In fact, several are very seldom seen by hobbyists.

At first appearance, some hatchlings of some water monitors are confusingly similar to babies of the African Nile monitor. When they are viewed critically, however, one sees many differences. Perhaps the most diagnostic difference is the position of the nostril. This is about equidistant from the eye and the tip of the snout on Nile monitors, and close to the tip of the snout on the various water monitors.

Hatchlings within the water monitor group may be black, olive black, or deep olive brown. They may be either liberally or sparsely marked with bands and ocelli of yellow ochre, bright yellow, or chalk white. The light markings are more profuse on the sides than on the dorsum. Hatchlings and juveniles are more prominently patterned than adults.

Adult water monitors tend to assume an olive-brown to deep brown ground coloration that is

Varanus cumingi *is a pale colored Philippine water monitor.*

patterned with lighter crossbands and ocelli. The markings may vary from well defined to obscure.

By affixing invalid names to imported water monitors, the pet industry has contributed to the nomenclatural confusion surrounding this species complex of monitors. Although it is invalid, dealers use the name *V. salvator komaini* for big, predominantly black water monitors from unknown provenance; there is no such subspecies, a big clue that the dealer has no idea what is being offered—or doesn't want you to know.

The widely flung Philippine Islands are home to several species of water monitor. One of the prettiest is the rather small *V. cumingi*. The babies are brilliantly patterned with orange dorsal and lateral spots, an orange head, and orange nape stripes against an olive-brown ground coloration. Although the colors fade with growth, even adult cumingi retain a degree of patterning unusual in other races.

At least two other species, both less brightly colored than *V. cumingi*, also occur on the Philippines. These are *V. marmoratus* and *V. s. nuchalis*. These two lizards seem marginally distinct from each other, being differentiated by the comparative size of the enlarged nape scales.

None of the Philippine species of water monitor is common in the pet trade. *V. togianus*, a dark, poorly known race from the Sulawesi, is even less frequently seen than the Philippine species.

It is the nominate race, *V. s. salvator*, that is best known to both herpetologists and herpetoculturists and has the widest range. This race appears over much of Southeast Asia, on Irian Jaya, and on many Indonesian islands.

The term *water monitor* refers more to the habits of the adult than to those of the juveniles (which tend to be very arboreal). Such habitat

An alert juvenile Asian water monitor.

partitioning of the varying sizes helps prevent cannibalism.

Some water monitor species have been captive bred, but most of those in the world pet trade were collected from the wild. As many as two dozen eggs are laid, and the most successful incubation temperature seems to be between 83 and 86°F (28–30°C). Incubation duration is upward of six months.

In keeping with their strongly arboreal tendencies, the babies of the water monitor are highly insectivorous. Tree-climbing crabs, snails, and other such invertebrates are also consumed. Baby water monitors also eat smaller lizards, snakes, and tree frogs, and would certainly not be averse to a meal of nestling birds or bird eggs, should the opportunity arise.

If hungry, an adult water monitor will eat anything it can overpower. These lizards have been observed testing air currents, apparently on the trail of odoriferous carrion. Fish, mammals, turtles, hatchling crocodiles, and the eggs of birds and reptiles are favored foods.

The freckled monitor, V. tristis orientalis, *is slender and attenuate.*

Unlike Nile monitors, which are noted for their foul dispositions, water monitors, if obtained young and worked with gently and diligently, can become very tame. One should always keep in mind, however, the terrible potential of those powerful jaws and claws. Until you are absolutely certain that the lizard is not only tame, but tame with you, exercise caution.

Housing a monitor of such proportions may tax the ingenuity of a private keeper, although the care will be greatly eased if the specimen is docile. In many cases, an entire room may be dedicated as a monitor enclosure. At the very least, an enclosure of 6 feet (2 m) in width and 12 feet (4 m) (about half room size) in length is needed to house an adult. Basking areas warmed to 90–96°F (31–35.5°C), a hide box, a very firmly affixed elevated shelf or tree trunk, and a large, easily cleaned water dish are the suggested cage furniture. Although a single properly positioned heating bulb will suffice for juvenile water monitors, several heat bulbs will probably be necessary to allow an adult to thermoregulate effectively. Be certain that the bulbs are placed so your lizard cannot come in direct contact with them and sufficiently far from the water receptacle so they do not get splashed by the lizard's movement.

Australian Monitors

Australia is the homeland of no fewer than 30 species of monitors (called *goannas* in Australia). Three subgenera, *Varanus, Euprepiosaurus,* and *Odatria*, are represented on the desert continent.

A fair number of species are now found in American herpetoculture, and several of them are being bred with regularity. Two of the smaller

Australian "Pygmy" Monitors

Subgenus *Odatria*

Varanus acanthurus ssp., ridge-tailed monitors, northern Australia

V. baritji, White's monitor, northern Northern Territory, Australia

V. brevicauda, short-tailed monitor, central and Western Australia

V. caudolineata, stripe-tailed monitor, Western Australia

V. eremius, rusty desert monitor, central and Western Australia

V. gilleni, pygmy mulga monitor, interior central and Western Australia

V. galuert, Glauert's monitor, northeastern Western Australia

V. glebopalma, long-tailed rock monitor, extreme northern Australia

V. kingorum, King's monitor, Kimberly Region of Western Australia

V. mitchelli, Mitchell's water monitor, extreme northern Australia

V. pellewensis, Pellew Islands monitor, Pellew Islands, Northern Territory, Australia

V. pilbarensis, Pilbara rock monitor, northwestern Western Australia

V. primordius, blunt-spined monitor, northern Northern Territory, Australia

V. scalaris, Australian spotted tree monitor, northern Australia

V. semiremix, rusty monitor, coastal eastern Queensland, Australia

V. similis, New Guinea spotted tree monitor, New Guinea

V. storri ssp., Storr's monitors, two disjunct populations in northern Australia

V. timorensis ssp., Timor and Roti Island monitors, Timor and Roti Islands

V. tristis ssp., mourning and freckled monitors, most of Australia

species—the ridge-tailed (*V. acanthurus* ssp.), and the Storr's (*V. storri* ssp.)—barely known to American hobbyists only a few years ago, are now actually commonly offered.

A few other species—the pygmy mulga monitor (*V. gilleni*), the Timor monitor (*V. timorensis*), the rusty monitor (*V. kingorum*), Gould's monitor (*V. gouldii* ssp.), the argus monitor (*V. panoptes* ssp.), and even the beautiful lace monitor (*V. varius*)—are also being bred by private hobbyists, but in very limited numbers. German hobbyists, seemingly far more advanced in the art of monitor breeding than their American counterparts, are producing at least small numbers of many additional species.

The Australian Ridge-Tailed Monitor

V. acanthurus ssp.

Once truly a rarity in the United States, the Australian ridge-tailed monitor, *V. acanthurus*, is now the species most frequently bred. Even so, prices for this saxicolous desert species remain very high in America. It is also being bred in Europe, but remains expensive there, too.

The ridge-tailed monitor is a beautiful spiny-tailed species that occasionally attains an adult size of 28 inches (71 cm). However, most seen in herpetoculture are well under that length. In fact, comparatively few will attain 20 inches (50 cm) in total length.

The pygmy mulga monitor, **V. gilleni,** *is now available to hobbyists.*

Unlike many of the monitors more frequently seen by hobbyists, the ridge-tailed monitor does not have a long, slender, whiplike tail. The tail of *V. acanthurus* is rather short (approximately 1.5 times the snout–vent length), heavy, and prominently whorled with spiny, keeled scales. The ground color of the lizard is olive brown. There are light longitudinal stripes on the nape and sides of the neck. Irregularly arranged light ocelli or spots on the trunk cause intricate reticulations of the dark pigment. Light rings alternate with dark on the tail. The rings are best defined on the basal three-fifths of the tail length.

This species is found over much of the arid and semiarid northern half of Australia in deeply creviced escarpments and on stony plains. Besides the deep rock fissures they prefer, spiny-tailed monitors seek protection beneath and between piled and jumbled boulders.

The Australian ridge-tailed monitor is represented by three rather poorly defined subspecies. The subspecies most commonly seen in the pet trade in America is also supposedly the most

brightly colored. This is the nominate form, *V. a. acanthurus.* It occurs over much of northwestern Australia. The eastern race, *V. a. brachyurus*, is grayer and less brightly patterned. A very dark race, *V. a. insulanicus*, occurs only on Groot Eylandt (an island east of Arnhem Land, Northern Territory, in the Gulf of Carpentaria).

Although a desert/arid-land lizard, captive ridge-tailed monitors seem able to adapt to many differing conditions. They are not only being bred in fairly large numbers by private hobbyists in the semiarid southwestern United States, but have been bred in quasi-natural conditions in perpetually humid southwestern Florida as well.

Our breeding colonies in southwest Florida were maintained in the aluminum rings described earlier. We created at least two equally high basking stations (one for each male in each cage) that extended to the top of the aluminum or above it. Besides each pinnacle serving as the center of a territory for a male, the monitors that used these elevated stations were then able to keep a wary eye out for approaching preda-

A trio of ridge-tailed monitors use their basking platform.

tors (which included their keepers). Despite their wariness, they were not as quick to disappear into the safety of their maze of boulders as some other monitor species.

This is another of the monitors that uses tripodal posturing to enable it to see a greater distance. We have not seen the males indulge in territorial displays while in the tripodal stance, but because many other monitor species display in this manner, ridge-tails probably do also.

We quickly learned that these monitors were sun worshippers. They might initially leave their refugia on warm, overcast days, but if startled they would again secrete themselves, seldom to venture forth again until the following day. On cool, overcast days the monitors were seldom seen at all. In keeping with many other heliotherms, on hot sunny days the ridge-tailed monitors basked in the morning and evening, retreating to their lairs during the very hottest hours. During these times, the basking rock surfaces might exceed 120°F (39°C). On cool days the acanthurus would bask throughout the day.

They required no additional winter heating while outside in southwest Florida. During the coldest weather these monitors retired to their burrows and remained (often for days) until they sensed warmer weather had returned.

If kept indoors, ridge-tails need to be kept warm. During the summer months, daytime highs of 88 to 94°F (31–34°C)—with a warmed basking spot of 106–110°F (41–43°C)—is suggested. Nighttime temperatures may be allowed to drop into the low 70sF (21–23°C). Ambient winter temperatures may be a few degrees cooler, but the superheated daytime basking area should be retained.

Although territorial, more than a single male of this species can usually be kept with several females if the caging is large enough and the cage furniture is properly arranged to provide an elevated perch and hiding area for each male.

HELPFUL HINT: Ridge-tailed monitors are good candidates for outdoor caging in tropical areas.

Once a rarity, the ridge-tailed monitor, V. acanthurus *ssp., is now the most popular of the dwarf Australian species.*

If you provide UVA and UVB lighting with one of the new incandescent UVHeat bulbs, only one male can be housed per cage.

Egg size and egg quantity may vary with the size of the female monitor. Maximum clutch size is often quoted as five, and the hatchlings are said to be "tiny" (total length of 2.5 inches [6.3 cm]); Sprackland 1992). However, we have had clutches from large females number up to eight eggs and the hatchlings somewhat more than 4 inches (10 cm) in total length. Admittedly, this is smaller than the small Storr's monitor, but it is larger than often reported.

Our eggs were incubated in slightly dampened sphagnum and hatched in 81 to 90 days at "room temperature"—82–90°F (28–32°C).

Hatchlings began feeding on insects within 24 hours. A diet of commercially procured crickets, mealworms, waxworms, and butterworms was augmented with netsful of "field plankton" (insects that were netted locally in nearby insec-

ticide-free, vacant grassy fields). Adults also ate pinky mice readily.

Storr's Monitor
V. storris sp.

Although certainly not yet a commonly seen species, the attractive little spiny-tailed Storr's monitor, *V. storri*, has been bred in small numbers in the United States for more than 15 years. It is a rather common monitor in two disjunct areas of Australia. One population (*V. s. storri*) is present in northwestern Queensland and adjacent Northern Territory. The second population (*V. s. ocreatus*) occurs in northeastern Western Australia and adjacent Northern Territory.

Between these two populations, one enters the range of a look-alike species, currently identified as *V. primordius*.

The taxonomic status of primordius is uncertain. It differs from storri only in the number of scales encircling the midbody, primordius with 69 or fewer, storri, 71 or more, and in color—primordius is often a little darker. Storri-primordius hybrids muddy the taxonomic waters even more.

V. storri is reddish-tan with a fine (but vague) pattern of darker reticulations. The spiny tail of *V. storri* is unpatterned.

Storr's monitors are reportedly 12 inches (30 cm), but most are smaller. These are rock-dwelling monitors with a tail somewhat greater in length than the combined head and body length. They are hardy and easily kept.

Although we initially kept our colony of Storr's monitors indoors, we soon added an out-side pen for them, like that provided for the ridge-tailed monitors. Besides using the under-ground refugia, the Storr's monitors dug lengthy burrows of their own. Occasionally these were started at the base of a boulder, but more often the lizards dug horizontally outward from an open side of the prepared underground refugia. These tunnels measured up to a yard (1 m) and were wide enough at the end to allow the lizard to reverse its position.

The interactions between members of the storri group were interesting. The males were somewhat, but not persistently, territorial, usu-ally satisfying themselves with posturing and threats rather than actual skirmishes. Each rock pile was the display site for one male. The pinna-cle rock of each of the piles was somewhat below the top of the 2-foot (.6-m) aluminum restraining wall of the enclosure. Because of this, the light of the rising sun would reach one of the piles a few minutes before it reached the other, and the rays of the setting sun would linger on another pile for a few minutes longer

A portrait of a Storr's monitor.

than on the other two. The monitors soon learned this. All would clamber from their night-time refugia when the sun began to warm the aluminum wall of the enclosure to claim their respective rock pile. As the warming rays reached the first of the pinnacles, the females would all join that male to begin their daily regimen of basking. However, if the two males who had staked out the other piles attempted to approach, they were met by the resident male with threats and feints. These involved inflating or flattening his body, extending his legs, inflat-ing the throat (gular) area, and shaking his head from side to side, nose down.

The threats worked. No matter how much they wished to sun, the other males would scuttle away. But these two males soon learned another ploy that seemed to work as well for them. By assuming a tripodal stance—anterior almost fully erect—they could benefit from the sun at almost the same time the monitor across the cage did, and, because they were at home on their own rock piles, they experienced no aggressive inter-actions. In the evening, since the shadows would reach his rock pile first, the early-sun male would assume the tripodal stance and gain an additional few minutes of sunlight. In the several

years that we had these interesting dwarf monitors, we never saw a female assume a tripodal position.

On overcast days, when temperatures were below 75°F (24°C), these monitors seldom emerged from their refugia. Even on warmer, cloudy days their appearance above ground was often sporadic. On the other hand, if the sun was shining strongly, these monitors emerged from their refugia even on cold days, when air temperatures were in the 40s and 50sF (4–12°C). During such weather conditions they basked virtually all day long. And on sunny days during our hot summers, when air temperatures would often near or reach 95°F (35°C)—the midafternoon surface temperature of the rock formations would hover at 120°F (49°C)—the Storr's monitors would bask in early morning and late afternoon, retiring to the coolness of their refugia when temperatures were the hottest.

For indoor caging, summer daytime temperatures should vary from 88 to 94°F (31–34°C), with a brightly illuminated basking area of from 106 to 110°F (41–43°C). Nighttime temperatures can drop into the low 70sF (22°C). Winter temperatures a few degrees cooler may assist in reproductive cycling. The superwarmed daytime basking area should be retained. Photoperiods should also be lessened somewhat during the winter months.

We successfully bred V. s. storri for the first time in 1981. This was, to our knowledge, the first time the species had been bred in captivity. They have since been captive bred both in the United States and Europe.

One female, found inexplicably dead in her outside cage, contained six fully shelled but still premature eggs. A few days later, on a morning after a very cold night, a pair of desiccated eggs was found near the mouth of a burrow. They were too desiccated and chilled to revitalize.

A single "good" egg was found at the cul-de-sac end of the foot-long (.3-m) burrow, beneath a torpid female storri. The egg was removed for incubation indoors. A closed margarine tub was used. The incubation medium was barely dampened sphagnum, but the humidity within the closed container was retained at 100 percent. At a temperature that fluctuated from 82 to 90°F (28–32°C), the egg hatched in 80 days.

Measuring 5³⁄₁₆ inches (13 cm) in overall length, the hatchling, which was precisely like the adults in coloration and pattern, was comparatively huge. The yolk sac had been fully used during incubation, and by the day after its hatching, the monitor was eagerly consuming crickets and other insects.

The growth of the hatchling was rapid, and the lizard was fully grown at about eight months of age. Additional hatchlings in subsequent years confirmed most initial findings.

Although the adults of Storr's monitors were primarily insectivorous, eating crickets, caterpillars, grasshoppers, waxworms, and June beetles, they readily consumed the occasional pinky mice offered them. They also lapped eagerly at a honey-pureed fruit mixture that we prepared for our day geckos and once offered to them on a whim. They liked it so much that we continued to offer it to them periodically. Large shallow dishes of water were always available, but we never saw Storr's monitors do more than drink from them. After initially scattering as we approached, Storr's monitors also drank droplets of water copiously from the rocks and plants when their enclosure was misted.

A portrait of the pygmy mulga monitor.

Because of its diminutive size and overall hardiness, we consider the Storr's one of the finest of the occasionally available small monitor lizards.

A Few Eagerly Sought but Hard-to-Acquire Monitors

The pygmy mulga monitor, *V. gilleni*, is a slender arboreal and saxicolous (rock-dwelling) species of the arid interior of the Australian continent. It is gray anteriorly, on the lower sides, and on the tail and reddish dorsally. The dark dorsal and basal tail marking are coalesced into vaguely delineated crossbars, and the distal tail markings are rather well-defined longitudinal stripes. Once rarely seen outside of its native country, the pygmy mulga monitor has now been bred by both American and European hobbyists and zoos. It is occasionally available from specialist dealers.

The Timor Monitor
V. timorensis ssp.

The Timor monitor, *V. timorensis*, is rather readily available in the pet trades of America and Europe at what is, for a small, coveted monitor, a moderate price. Two forms are being imported—one blackish with gold ocelli (some are dull and almost unicolored) and the other, although also variable, often blackish with a pattern of white to gray spots and ocelli (and seemingly a slightly different tail scalation).

The former is the nominate form of the species and is classified as *V. t. timorensis*. This race occurs on the island of Timor, its satellite islands, and New Guinea.

The latter form, long scientifically known as *V. t. similis*, is now being considered a full species by many researchers.

If named as a full species, the designation of *timorensis* is dropped and the lizard is referred to as *V. similis*. *V. t. similis* is a pretty monitor occurring in northeastern Australia and, ostensibly, southern New Guinea; from the latter location it is being exported in some numbers.

*The spotted tree monitor, **Varanus similis**, was once a subspecies of the Timor monitor.*

Varanus scalaris, *the banded tree monitor is a relative of the Timor monitor.*

A third subspecies, *V. t. scalaris* (also considered a full species, *V. scalaris*, by some researchers), is found in northwestern Australia. This, too, is a very pretty monitor, patterned with myriad small yellow spots on a dark, often nearly black ground. This form is not known to occur in captivity except in Australian collections.

Unless specified otherwise, the comments that follow apply specifically to our experience with *V. t. timorensis*, a monitor with which we worked for several years. However, they probably apply equally to both other subspecies.

The Timor is a small, slender, arboreal monitor that seldom attains 20 inches (50 cm) in total length. The long tail is at least 1.5 times the snout–vent length. It is a hardy species that has been bred in captivity on numerous occasions. The hatchlings are more brightly patterned than the adults; captives feed on a combination of insects, high-quality canned cat food, pinky mice, and beaten eggs.

We have found Timor monitors to be less cold tolerant than certain other monitors from similar latitudes. In fact, Timors often continued placidly sunning on hot days, long after other species had retreated to their refugia. Although we kept the Timors outdoors throughout the year in southwest Florida, we learned that it was necessary to warm their underground refugia with a heat tape when temperatures plummeted. We used 55°F (13°C) as an arbitrary temperature below which the heat tapes were activated.

If they are maintained indoors, we suggest that the same temperature regimen as for other small monitors be used:

Daytime summer	86–94°F (30–34°C)
Nighttime summer	70–80°F (21–27°C)
Daytime winter	78–86°F (25.5–30°C)
Nighttime winter	68–74°F (20–23°C)

A basking area warmed to 104–110°F (40–43°C) should be available during daytime throughout the year. A "normal" photoperiod (less in winter, more in summer) should be provided.

In the wild, these are highly arboreal monitors, which forage, rest, and probably breed in the trees. They are active and quick, characteristics that are carried over into captivity. Timor monitors are excellent jumpers, and are more adept at escaping their enclosures than many other monitor species. If these monitors are kept indoors, a large, vertically oriented cage should be provided.

We have also found that, since trees would be difficult for us to provide, Timor monitors adapt very well to life in rock piles. Those that we maintained never tamed, and were as ready to flee at our approach after several years in captivity as they were on the day they were received. We also found that these lizards had voracious appetites, and none was reluctant to eat half-grown or even larger mice, lizards such as anoles and skinks that wandered into their cage, and large and seemingly unpalatable beetles and bugs. They also readily consumed vitamin-and-mineral-enhanced canned cat foods of many flavors. A fairly large flat bowl of water was always available, and occasionally the Timor monitors entered and soaked for short periods. However, even when soaking, these lizards were always ready to dart for cover at the slightest disturbance.

While watching the interactions of male Timor monitors caged communally indoors, we thought them quite tolerant of each other. After moving the lizards to outside facilities, we were quickly disabused of this notion. Once in the natural unfiltered sunlight, the males became so agonistic toward each other that we could keep only one per 10-foot (3-m) diameter cage. The females remained amiable, however.

When displaying or apparently just trying to see for a longer distance, the males assumed a tripodal stance, standing upright on their rear legs while supported by their tails. If in a territorial dispute, while the lizards were erect, their bodies were either flattened and tilted toward the interloper or inflated. Their heads were angled downward, throats inflated, tongues extended for several seconds at a time, and the neck and anterior body moved in sinuous undulations. Males occasionally grappled while in this upright position. Aggression was also evident while the lizards were in their more normal four-footed posture. Then the body was inflated somewhat and flattened vertically, the body and neck were "humped," the gular area was inflated, and the head was held at a curious angle. The tongue was often extended for several seconds. The territorial dispute was usually settled without actual combat.

During the time that we had Timor monitors, we found two nests of eggs. One consisted of six, and the other of four eggs. The hatchlings were very slender, somewhat more brightly colored, voracious, 5-inch (13-cm) diminutive duplicates of the adults.

Besides those mentioned earlier, a few monitor species once considered rare, or at least unobtainable by private owners, are also available to hobbyists. Because of their dwindling numbers in nature, wild monitors will probably not be available in the pet trade for many more years. In the interim it is up to us to ferret out the secrets of their private lives. Only in this way will we ensure that any remain available for future hobbyists to enjoy.

HELPFUL HINT: The Timor monitors we housed in naturalistic outdoor settings seemed to be much more alert and unapproachable than many other monitor species.

Crevice Monitor

V. kingorum

To get some idea of the appearance of *V. kingorum*, envision a Storr's monitor with a proportionately long, nonspinose tail. Although *V. kingorum* is being bred by a handful of private American and European hobbyists, it will remain a comparative rarity for many years, in part because of its origin—Australia—and its scarcity within Australia. It has been found only among fissured sandstone outcroppings and escarpments in the Kimberley region, basically at the junction of Western Australia and Northern Territory.

V. kingorum is a wary, seldom-seen monitor that is quick to retreat deeply into the safety of the fissures of its rock homeland when frightened. The long tail accounts for nearly two-thirds of this species' 15-inch (38-cm) total length. The caudal scales are heavily keeled, but not spinose. The reddish dorsum is patterned with vaguely delineated irregular darker markings in the form of ocelli, rosettes, or simple spots, several scales in size. On the distal two-thirds of the tail the spots may form vague broken stripes.

Gould's Monitor

V. gouldii

Of the Australian monitors, the large Gould's monitor, *V. gouldii*, is the best known to the general populace. Also called the sand monitor (or goanna), this is the species most often seen on TV screens, grappling in territorial disputes, careening off in bipedal bursts of speed, or standing partially or virtually erect in a tripodal defensive or scanning position. When the stance is assumed for defensive purposes, the gular area is prominently distended and the

Australian Desert Monitors and Relatives

Subgenus *Varanus*

V. giganteus, Perentie, interior Queensland to coastal Western Australia

V. gouldii ssp., Gould's monitors and sand monitors, most of Australia and southern New Guinea

V. komodensis, Komodo monitor, Seychelles Islands

V. mertensi, Merten's water monitor, coastal northern Australia

V. panoptes ssp., argus monitors, two disjunct populations. Most of northern Australia and central Western Australia

V. rosenbergi, Rosenberg's monitor, extreme southern Australia

V. spenceri, Spencer's monitor, interior Queensland and Northern Territory, Australia

V. varius, lace monitor, eastern Australia

tongue lolls. When standing merely to observe its surroundings, the throat is not distended, and the tongue is actively protruded and withdrawn.

V. gouldii is found in arid or subarid habitats over all the Australian continent, except for the extreme southeast. It attains a total length of about 5 feet (1.5 m). The tail, which is about one and a half times the snout–vent length, is heavy, and used with lashlike efficiency against approaching adversaries. Rounded basally, the distal half of the tail is laterally compressed and has paired dorsal keels. In keeping with their largely terrestrial habits, Gould's monitors are a heavy-bodied species, even more so after a sizable meal.

A Gould's monitor watches the camera.

These monitors seem most at home in or near considerable ground cover, and even the most brightly colored among them virtually disappear when sitting quietly amidst the dappled shade of a desert thicket. They are of variable ground color, but they are usually similar in color to the desert sands over which they race.

The specimens from Australia's arid, red sand desert interior are known subspecifically as *V. g. flavirufus.* They tend to have bright reds, russets, and yellows incorporated into their dorsal colors. Because most hobbyists think this is the prettier subspecies, and because it is the more uncommon in collections, it is particularly coveted.

V. g. gouldii is more variable. It may be an almost unicolored tan or olive brown or strikingly patterned in transverse rows of large cream spots against a nearly black ground color.

Both subspecies have an often prominent dark temporal stripe, and both tend to have a light, unmarked tail tip. The young of both subspecies tend to be the brightest, whereas older *V. g. gouldii* tend toward the dullest coloration and least pattern.

Merten's water monitor in profile.

Although it is well represented in both private collections and zoos of the world, the Gould's monitor is still too uncommonly seen to be considered popular. It has been bred on several occasions, both by American and European herpetoculturists.

Despite its large size, the Gould's monitor seems to produce a comparatively small clutch of rather large eggs. The count most frequently mentioned varies from four and eight. This small maximum number may be attributed as much to a lack of research as to actuality.

Merten's Water Monitor
V. mertensi

The 4-foot (1.2-m) length of the males of Merten's water monitor, *V. mertensi*, makes them dramatically larger than their mates.

Besides size differences, a difference in "face" coloration often occurs. Sexually mature males develop a blue suffusion to the sides of the face, and the females develop a pale orange facial blush. The overall ground color is olive gray to

HELPFUL HINT: Merten's is one of the very few monitor species in which sexual dimorphism is pronounced.

This is a hatchling Merten's water monitor, V. mertensi.

olive brown or black. Tiny yellow spots are present on the posterior nape, the trunk, limbs, and tail. This is a highly aquatic species that spends a great deal of time in the water and most of the remaining time very near it.

In keeping with its water-dwelling habits, the Merten's feeds on crustaceans, mollusks, and fish as well as the "usual" monitor fare. Although small numbers of this species are regularly bred, incubation or other problems have resulted in

poor hatches and malformed young. Research continues.

This species occurs along watercourses in the northern quarter of Australia.

Argus Monitor
V. panoptesis

Because of its intricate pattern of eyelike spots, *V. panoptesis* is often referred to as the argus monitor. There are three currently recognized subspecies, *panoptes* and *rubidus* of Australia, and *horni* of New Guinea.

This is one of the most beautiful and intricately patterned of the larger Australian/New Guinean monitors. Until 1980, this species was thought to be merely one of the many color phases of the widespread and variable Gould's monitor. The argus monitor tops out at about 4 feet (1.2 m) in length, a slightly smaller adult

Argus monitors have vividly delineated facial stripes.

The argus monitor, V. panoptes horni, is quite like the Gould's monitor in appearance.

size than that attained by the very similar Gould's monitor. The tail of the argus monitor, which is rounded basally and strongly compressed, is about 1.5 times the snout–vent length. The tail bears two prominent dorsal keels.

If it is threatened and escape seems difficult, the argus monitor inflates its throat and lolls the tongue out. It may use this defensive display while either in the normal four-footed stance or, after assuming a tripodal position, propped erect on rear legs and tail. While still on all fours, the argus monitor will also lash an adversary strongly with its tail. If escape becomes possible, the lizard will dash off, first on all fours and then becoming bipedal as it speeds up.

In Australia, the pretty yellow-spangled Panoptes has a much smaller range than does *V. gouldii.* As far as is currently known, the ranges of the two subspecies are widely separated. However, the presence in collections of a very few specimens from intermediate areas between the main ranges suggests that additional observation would benefit our knowledge. *V. p. panoptes* occurs over the northern fifth of Australia. It is the darker form and is often patterned with bands of discrete yellow spots

arranged in regular to irregular fashion. Prominent-to-obscure bands of smaller black spots often alternate between the yellow. Other specimens are liberally peppered with light scales among the dark and have well-defined light ocelli haphazardly scattered over both dorsal and lateral surfaces. The tail is banded to the tip.

V. p. rubidus is the race encountered in coastal and inland central Western Australia. Although the pattern is quite similar to that of the nominate race, the dorsal and lateral surfaces of this subspecies are usually washed with sand red and the terminal one-fifth of the tail is straw yellow to cream and unbanded.

Range alone will identify the southern New Guinean *V. p. horni.* This is fortunate, for this race is very like the Australian *V. p. panoptes* in overall appearance. The majority of the specimens seen in the pet trade of the United States are shipped from New Guinea.

V. panoptes is an active monitor. Although primarily terrestrial, it can climb if necessary and is perfectly able to swim. It seems more predisposed to mesic (an area with moderate moisture) and riparian habitats than the Gould's monitor. This species has been bred by European hobbyists.

INTRODUCTION TO THE TEIIDS

The family Teiidae, the teiids, include the tegus, caiman lizards, race runners, whiptails, and several lesser-known genera, all of New World origin.

The members of this family range in size from just 1½ to 48 inches (3.7–125 cm). These lizards may be stout to slender. Usually the snout is pointed and the tail fragile. They are much more abundant in the West Indies and Latin America than in North America. The United States is home to just one genus, *Aspidoscelis,* the racerunners and whiptails.

Teiids are quite similar in appearance but vastly dissimilar in size. Only one genus, *Tupinambis,* is well represented in the American pet trade.

Like the monitors, many of these lizards may rise onto their hind legs to see above obstructions. When in this position, their tails are used as supports. Besides this tripodal stance, teiids are fully capable of running bipedally when startled. In addition to being collected alive for

the pet industry, the larger teiids are killed for their skins. The tanned skins are used for boots and shoes, hatbands, and wallets.

Diet and behavior: Teiids are generally very adept at finding insects and other prey. Fruits and palm nuts are also readily eaten by some species. These lizards fully use not only visual, but tactile and chemo-sensory prey location techniques. It is likely that auditory cues play a part in prey location, for teiids are able to locate, then unearth, burrowing beetle larvae that seem to be making no visible signs on the surface.

A rapid scratching with the front feet is used to uncover subterranean prey once it is located.

A similar scratching motion, but this time with just a single foot waved above the surface of the ground, is used to indicate nervousness (as immediately before a dash to safety) and as a territorial signal to an approaching interloping male.

The Argentine tegu tames well.

The Species of Tegus

Tupinambis duseni, yellow tegu (considered
   T. rufescens by some authorities),
   Paraguay
T. longilineus, Rondonia lined tegu, central
   Brazil
T. merinanae, black and white tegu,
   temperate southern Brazil, Argentina,
   Uruguay
T. quadrilineatus, Four-lined tegu, west
   central Brazil
T. rufescens, red tegu, Paraguay, Argentina,
   southern Brazil
T. teguixin, Amazonian tegu, Amazonian
   provinces of South America
T. species Cf teguixin, blue tegu, Colombian
   black and white tegu, Colombia

Despite being thought of as terrestrial lizards,
many species, including the tegus and caiman
lizards, have been observed foraging in trees,
and the nests of some have been found exca-
vated into arboreal termitaria. When not foraging in trees, the caiman lizard spends its time in
rivers, and is considered to be semi-aquatic.

Teiids are as adept at noting and defining
potential danger as they are at foraging. Their
dashes to safety are often along established
trails. All are accomplished burrowers, usually
constructing lengthy home burrows to which
they regularly return.

Tegus

Tupinambis sp.

It is the tegus that are most sought by both
casual hobbyists and herpetoculturists. Tegus
are easily recognized because in gross external
appearance they resemble a heavy-bodied, big-
headed monitor lizard.

Tegus differ greatly from the monitors in the
arrangement of the body and tail scalation. A
tegu's dorsal scales are shiny, relatively small,
and flattened. The 20 to 40 rows of belly scales
are large, platelike, and regularly arranged. The
tail is round in cross section and has no keel,
and the scales are arranged in prominent
whorls. Tegus are essentially terrestrial but are
able to climb.

Tegus have both femoral and preanal pores.
Males may be identified by the presence of a
small postanal spur on each side of the tail base.
The spurs are usually composed of three barely
protruding ventrolateral scales. Although small,
the spurs are easily visible if the lizard is in hand.

The adult black and yellow, black and white,
or red tegus can be mistaken for few other
lizards.

The huge black and white and the red tegus
are more cold tolerant than the other species.
This cold tolerance is understandable, because
these two species range much farther south–

Teiid in tripodal pose.

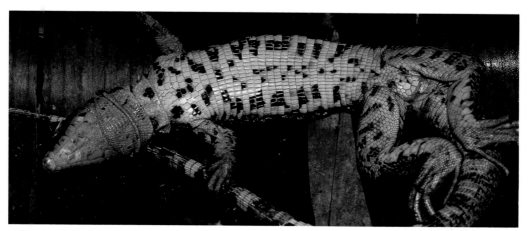

All tegus have large shiny plate-like scales on the belly.

ward (into the temperate regions of Argentina) than their congeners.

Breeding: Tegus of several species and color morphs are routinely bred in captivity. The lizards are most successfully bred when maintained outside in large cages where they can burrow. They are successfully kept and bred in outside facilities as far north as northern Florida and central Alabama.

Both the red and the black and white tegus seem to require a lengthy period of complete dormancy. This lengthy period of dormancy is very important if you hope to breed these lizards.

Both species cease feeding and begin preparing for dormancy while the weather is still quite warm. It will be necessary for you to consider this when making breeding preparations.

Amazon Tegus

In nature the Amazonian tegus (often referred to by hobbyists as Colombian golden, Colombian white, or Colombian blue tegus) are

active year-round. At (and near) the equator the hours of daylight and darkness vary only slightly through the calendar year. Seasons are defined by the amount of rainfall and varying humidity rather than by notable temperature changes. However, the activity period and reproductive biology of captive Amazonian tegus is apparently determined both by photoperiod and temperature/humidity. These tegus

A hatchling Amazonian tegu.

The blue tegu is gaining quickly in hobbyist popularity.

may choose to become dormant during the winter months, or they may simply become less active and feed more sparingly.

The ambient maintenance temperature for Amazonian tegus should be lowered slightly during the shortened days of late autumn and winter. Nonetheless, a warmed basking site (90–110°F [32–44°C]) should be provided daily. Night temperatures should be 70-75°F (21–24°C). The nighttime temperature drops are usually easily accomplished when the basking light is turned off.

Because imported specimens have remained readily available and inexpensive, Amazonian tegus have served as the introductory tegu for many hobbyists. Low cost and ready availability, however, do not mean that the lizard will readily adapt to captivity and humans. This is certainly the case with most imported Amazonian tegus—especially with wild-collected adults. These large—commonly to 3 feet (1 m)—and

HELPFUL HINT: Teiids can actually hear their prey underground.

powerful lizards usually remain "flighty," will scratch with their claws and whip with their tails if handled, and will bite savagely and void excrement on their handler if carelessly restrained. This is not exactly an ideal set of characteristics for a budding hobbyist to encounter. However, if obtained while young and handled frequently and carefully, black and yellow tegus can become quite tractable.

Because imported, typically colored (black and gold) Amazonian tegus remain inexpensive, no extensive efforts have been made by herpetoculturists to breed them. However, the blue phase is bred extensively. In fact, albinos of two forms, snows, and hybrids between the blue and the red tegus, have been developed.

Occasional wild-collected female Amazonian tegus, gravid when collected, may lay a clutch of eggs. An incubation temperature of 83–86°F (28–30°C) will result in hatchlings emerging in approximately 120 to more than 170 days, a much longer incubation duration than is known for other more temperate tegu species. This lengthy incubation period is difficult to explain, for of all the tegus, the climatic conditions at

Red tegus are very cold tolerant.

the latitude near the equator where this tegu occurs seem the most equable for rapid incubation. Perhaps embryonic development temporarily ceases during the dry season. Such a diapause is well documented in other reptiles.

Red and Argentine Tegus

In the United States, the two most commonly bred tegu species are the red and the black and white. Should you decide to set up an outside facility, remember that tegus are powerful lizards; they are efficient diggers, can climb reasonably well, and will constantly investigate the walls of their cage for weakened areas. These lizards can and will swim.

Winter protection must be provided for tegus maintained outside. If the lizards are unable to dig hibernating burrows, a hide box/hibernaculum heated to a temperature of 66-70°F (18–21°C) should be provided. Agama International of Montevallo, Alabama, is one the largest breeders of both black and white

and red tegus. They allow their adult tegus to burrow to a depth of 2 feet (.6 m). The tegus hibernate communally.

In both cases, the lizards' appetites begin to drop off in the early autumn and the lizards cease feeding shortly thereafter. Because cold weather comes to Alabama earlier and lasts longer than it does in southern Florida, the black and white tegus at Agama International hiber-

Red tegus, **T. rufescens,** *attain a large size and heavy girth.*

Amazonian tegus, T. teguixin, *are not at all cold tolerant.*

nate for the longer time. Owners Bert and Hester Langerwerf estimate that their black and white tegus eat about four and a half months of the twelve, are active for about another month and a half, and are in actual hibernation for at least six months of the year. Perhaps it is the waning photoperiod that dictates the activity cycle of the Langerwerfs' tegus, for the animals prepare and retire to their hibernacula while daytime temperatures are still in the upper 80sF (31°C).

In southwest Florida Chuck Hurt noted that red tegus are inactive for about three and a half months out of each year. Like the black and whites, the red tegus cease feeding a few weeks before actually beginning their hibernation.

The lizards breed shortly after emerging from hibernation. Female tegus are quite unlike most other lizards, because they actually construct a nest of leaves, straw, and other ground debris to accommodate their eggs. In captivity, the

HELPFUL HINT: Teiids forage for prey, rather than pursue it.

observed females nudged and dragged the provided nesting material under their enclosure shelters, constructing bulky nests before egg deposition.

Hurt provided a covered, earth-filled nesting box for the red tegus, a system that proved entirely acceptable to the big lizards. The clutches, all containing 20 to 25 eggs, have hatched in 77 to 92 days at an average incubation temperature of 84°F (29°C). The hatchlings measured nearly 10 inches (25 cm) in total length and, although not brightly colored, were attractive. With brownish-red and black crossbands, the hatchlings were of very different color from the hatchlings of either the Amazonian or the black and white tegus.

Red tegu adults, *T. rufescens*, are variably colored. This is especially so if you consider the Paraguayan tegu merely a color variant. In general, they are black lizards with profuse-to-sparse light markings. The light areas may be yellow to red on Paraguayan specimens, and just on the reddish side of white or actually quite a bright red on Argentine examples. Adult

Hatchling Argentine tegus may have considerable green on the nape.

males are usually a much brighter red than the females and may actually have even much of the black suffused with red. The color of the light bands of the females may vary from a muddy brown to cream brown, but is seldom truly red.

Besides being large—30 to about 40 inches (75–100 cm)—the red tegu is of robust build. Despite their large size, red tegus are relatively gentle lizards and are quick to accept humans as nonthreatening entities. Some specimens can actually be called tame.

Hurt has noted that the disposition of the relatively placid gravid females became increasingly agonistic as the laying date neared.

The black and white tegu, *T. merianae,* is arguably the longest of the tegus. Specimens of 4 feet (1.2 m) in length have been reported. Like the red tegu, the black and white tegu attains a great bulk with advancing age.

The Langerwerfs noted the same increase in agonistic behavior with their gravid female black and white tegus. As the laying date approached, the tegus become formidably aggressive.

The conditions provided at Agama International for the breeding of their black and white tegus are somewhat more "natural" than most captive conditions. The Langerwerfs provided loose straw and found that the females used it when contructing their nests.

The female black and white tegus dug deeply, lining the nesting chamber with straw. They then laid and covered the eggs and made an "attendance" chamber above the eggs. One female was tightly coiled in the top chamber when found by the Langerwerfs found her. She was protecting her clutch of 52 eggs!

At 80 to 85°F (27–29°C) incubation lasted about 65 days. The hatchlings of the black and white tegu are suffused dorsally and laterally

If you have a large enough cage, red tegus make hardy and attractive pets.

with bright green. This distinctive color fades rapidly and may be gone entirely after the second shedding.

T. merianae ranges widely over temperate southern and subtropical South America. It is known from Argentina, Brazil, and Uruguay.

Despite their great size, even the adults of tegus are alert, easily startled lizards. We have met the Amazonian tegu in forest clearings and

A portrait of a young Argentine tegu,
T. merinae.

along forest edges in Venezuela, Colombia, and Peru, and marveled at how unapproachable the big lizards were. Although we were still binocular-distance away, the basking adults would come to attention. A few more steps on our part and the anterior of the body would be lifted. Once that happened it took only a gentle movement from us—in any direction—to send the lizards cascading headlong into the surrounding forest. We could hear their retreat long after they had disappeared from sight. The closest we ever got to one in the wild was when we surprised a black and yellow tegu on the far side of a log over which we were stepping. The big lizard reacted with gaping jaws and slashing tail. It fled a short distance and disappeared into a burrow (probably of its own making) at the base of a shrub.

Most tegus make hardy pets, but those imported as adults will resist any efforts at taming.

A young female Argentine tegu.

Habitat/Caging

Because of their great adult size, tegus require large caging facilities. Many people allow a tame tegu the run of a room. In the hotter southerly climes, tegus are often kept in screened rooms or pool areas. If the screen goes all the way to the ground, you will have to reinforce it to assure that your lizard is restrained. Indoors, many are kept in cages that incorporate a full sheet of plywood as the bottom.

Although not particularly agile climbers, tegus have been reported in arboreal situations. This fact, plus their ability to jump upward, must be considered when their caging is being designed. Although a simple interior overhang will prevent their escape from a cage with suitably tall sides, a full cage cover remains the best way to assure containment of your tegus.

Daytime cage temperatures should be in the 77 to 85°F (25–29°C) range, with an illuminated basking area of 95 to 110°F (35–44°C) on one end. Night temperatures may be allowed to drop somewhat.

Tegus are opportunistic feeders both in nature and in captivity. Rodents, insects, nestling birds, some vegetation, and some prepared foods are accepted. Tegus seem to prefer succulent fruit over leafy vegetables.

Hatchlings require meals of healthy, gut-loaded mealworms, crickets, butterworms, silkworms, and pinky mice. Vitamin D3 and calcium additives should be provided three times weekly.

Tegus require fresh water, and if their dish is large enough, they may submerge, then curl up contentedly and soak for hours. They may also defecate in their water dish, so water quality must be closely monitored.

agonistic aggressive or defensive behavior

allopatric not occurring together but often in adjacent geographic areas

ambient temperature the temperature of the surrounding environment

anterior toward the front

anus the external opening of the cloaca; the vent

arboreal tree-dwelling

autotomize to use the ability to break easily or cast off (and usually regenerate) a part of the body, as in tail breakage in lizards

caudal pertaining to the tail

cloaca the common chamber into which digestive, urinary, and reproductive systems empty and that itself opens through the vent or anus

con— as used here, a prefix indicating "the same"; (*congeneric* refers to species in the same genus; *conspecific* indicates the same species)

deposition as used here, the laying of eggs

deposition site the spot chosen by the female to lay her eggs

dichromatic two color phases of the same species, often sex linked

dimorphic a difference in form, build, or coloration in the same species; often sex linked

diurnal active in the daytime

dorsal pertaining to the back; upper surface

dorsolateral pertaining to the upper sides

dorsum the upper surface

endemic confined to a specific region

estivation a period of warm-weather inactivity, often triggered by excessive heat or drought

form an identifiable species or subspecies

fracture planes softer areas in the tail vertebrae that allow the tail to break easily if seized

genus a classification of a group of species having similar characteristics. The genus falls between the next broader designation of "family" and the next narrower designation of "species."

Generais the plural of *genus*. The generic name is always capitalized and italicized.

gravid the reptilian equivalent of mammalian pregnant

gular pertaining to the throat

heliothermic pertaining to a species that basks in the sun to thermoregulate

hemipenes the dual copulatory organs of male lizards and snakes

hemipenis the singular form of *hemipenes*

hibernaculum a temperature-controlled shelter occupied during the winter by a dormant lizard

hybrid offspring resulting from the breeding of two species

hydrate to restore body moisture by drinking or absorption

insular as used here, island-dwelling intergrade offspring from the breeding of two subspecies

Jacobson's organ highly enervated sensory pits in the palate of snakes and lizards

juvenile a young or immature specimen

keel a ridge (along the center of a scale)

labial pertaining to the lips

lateral pertaining to the side

littoral seashore or seaside

melanism a profusion of black pigment, darker than normal

middorsal pertaining to the middle of the back

midventral pertaining to the center of the belly or abdomen

monotypic containing but one type

morphology study of the form and structure of animals and plants

*Merten's water monitors both
sleep and bask on sturdy limbs.*

ocelli outlined eye-shaped markings on the skin

oviparous reproducing by means of eggs that
hatch after laying

poikilothermic a species with no internal body
temperature regulation; "cold-blooded"

posterior toward the rear

race a subspecies

riparian riverine habitats

saurian any of a suborder of reptiles including
the lizards

saxicolous rock-dwelling

species a group of similar creatures that produce viable young when breeding. The taxonomic designation is narrower than genus
and broader than subspecies

subcaudal beneath the tail

subspecies the subdivision of a species, a race
that may differ slightly in color, size, scalation, or other criteria

SVL snout–vent length

sympatric occurring in the same range without
interbreeding

taxonomy the science of classification of plants
and animals

terrestrial land-dwelling

thermoregulate to regulate body temperature
by choosing a warmer or cooler environment

tympanum the external eardrum

vent the external opening of the cloaca; the
anus

venter the underside of a creature; the belly

ventral pertaining to the undersurface or belly

ventrolateral pertaining to the sides of the
venter (belly)

Note: Other scientific definitions are contained
in the following two volumes:

Peters, James A. 1964. *Dictionary of Herpetology.* New York: Hafner Publishing Co.

Wareham, David C. 1993. *The Reptile and
Amphibian Keeper's Dictionary.* London:
Blandford.

Bibliography

Auffenberg, Walter. 1981. *Behavioral Ecology of the Komodo Monitor.* Gainesville, FL: University of Florida Press.

_____. 1988. *Gray's Monitor Lizard.* Gainesville, FL: University of Florida Press.

Avila-Pires, T.C.S. 1995. *Lizards of Brazilian Amazonia (Reptilia: Squamata).* Leiden, The Netherlands: National Natural History Museum.

Bennett, Daniel. 1993. "A Review of Some Literature Concerning the Rough-Necked Monitor Lizard, *Varanus rudicollis.*" *Reptilian* 1(9).

_____. 1994. "Dumeril's Monitor Lizard, *Varanus dumerilii.*" *Reptilian* 3(3).

_____. 1995. "The Water Monitor, Varanus salvator." *Reptilian* 3(8).

Boyer, Donal M., and W. E. Lamereaux. 1984. "Captive Reproduction and Husbandry of the Pygmy Mulga Monitor, *Varanus gilleni,* at the Dallas Zoo." Thurmont, MD.

Proceedings of the Seventh Annual Reptile Symposium on Captive Propagation and Husbandry.

Branch, Bill. 1990. *Bill Branch's Field Guide to the Snakes and Other Reptiles of Southern Africa.* Sanibel Island, FL: Ralph Curtis Publishing.

Cogger, Harold G. 1992. *Reptiles and Amphibians of Australia.* Ithaca, NY: Cornell/Comstock.

Eidenmuller, Berndt. 1995. "Successful Breeding of the Merten's Monitor Lizard, *Varanus mertensi.*" *The Vivarium* 7(2).

Hurt, C. 1995. "The Red Tegu." *Reptiles Magazine* 3(1).

Langerwerf, Bert. 1995. "Keeping and Breeding the Argentine Black and White Tegu, *Tupinambis teguixin.*" *The Vivarium* 7(3).

Linville, Paula. 1995. "Komodo Dragons and the National Zoo." *Reptiles* Magazine 3(8).

Sprackland, Robert G. 1992. *Giant Lizards.* Neptune City, NJ: TFH.

Walsh, Trooper, R. Rosscoe, G. Birchard. 1993. "Dragon Tales: The History, Husbandry and Breeding of Komodo Monitors at the National Zoological Park." *The Vivarium* 4(6).

Affinity Groups

Herpetoculture is no longer an obscure hobby. Hobbyists may be surprised to find how many others share their interests in keeping monitor, tegus, and related lizards. Detailed additional information can be as close as the closest fellow hobbyist. You can find other hobbyists through your local pet store, library, or university or community college, or online.

Another source of information is herpetology groups. There are groups of hobbyists in many

A lace monitor in profile.

large cities of the world, as well as professional societies such as the Society for the Study of Reptiles and Amphibians (SSAR). Tegus have no society of their own; the following are sources of information about monitors.

Varanid Information Exchange
8726D S. Sepulveda Boulevard, #243
Los Angeles, CA 90045

Magazines

Reptiles Magazine
P.O. Box 6050
Mission Viejo, CA 92690-6050

The Vivarium
Available by membership in the American Federation of Herpetoculturists
P.O. Box 300067
Escondido, CA 92030-0067

The highly aquatic Merten's water monitor spends a great deal of time in or near the water.

The following are professional journals—available only to members of the societies or, occasionally, through used-book sellers.

Herp Review, and a more scholarly journal, *Journal of Herpetology*, are available from the Society for the Study of Reptiles
    and Amphibians
Department of Zoology
Miami University
Oxford, OH 45056

Copeia (a technical journal)
Business Office
Department of Zoology
Southern Illinois University
Carbondale, IL 62901-6501

INDEX

Breeding 51–57
Caging 9–15, **12, 14**
Dragon
    Black **15**
    Komodo **32, 58**
Feeding and Watering 19–29
Glossary 106–107
Handling 31–37
Health 39–49
Monitor 59–95
    African 63–69
    Argus **94**, 94–95, **95**
    Asian/Indonesian 69–78
    Australian 82–89
    Bengal **53**
    Blue-tailed **78**, 79, **79**
        Yellow-spotted **77**
    Crevice 92
    Crocodile **10, 52**
    Dumeril's **24, 69, 70**
    Freckled **48, 82**
    Gould's **29, 43**, 92–93, **93**
    Gray's **20**
    Lace **35, 108**
    Mangrove **28, 61**
    Nile **50, 67**
    Ornate **34, 38, 67**
    Peach-throat 79
    Pygmy Mulga **84, 89**
    Ridge-tailed **85**, 83–86, **86**
    Rough-necked **71, 72**
    Savanna **11, 21, 32, 40**, 63–65
    Storr's 86–89, **87**
    Timor **30,** 89–91
    Tree 72–76
    Banded **90**
    Black **44, 75, 76**
    Emerald **74**
    Merten's **47, 93**, 93–94, **94, 107, 109**

Spotted **89**
Yellow **29, 76**
Understanding your 5–7
Water
    Asian **8, 33,** 79–82, **81**
    Philippine **80**
    White-headed **4**
    White-throated **18, 22, 54, 62, 63, 66**
Tegus 97–105
    Amazonian **6, 7, 99**, 99–101, **102**
    Black and white (Argentine) **96**, 101–105, **103, 104, 105**
    Blue **6, 100**
    Red **13, 27, 57, 101, 104**
Tupinambis
    merianae 101–105
    rufescens 101–105
    teguixin 99–101
Varanus
    acanthurus 83–86
    albigularis 65–67
    argus 94–95
    beccarii 73–77
    cumingi **80, 81**
    doreanus 79
    dumerilii **69,** 69–72
    exanthematicus 63–65
    gouldii 92–93
    indicus 77–78
    kingorum 92
    marmoratus 81
    melinus 76
    mertensi 93–94
    niloticus 67–69
    ornatus 67–69
    prasinus 73–77
    rudicollis 69–72
    salvator 81, 83
    timorensis 89–91
    togianus 81

About the Authors

R. D. Bartlett is a herpetologist who has authored more than 650 articles and ten books, and coauthored an additional 35 books. He lectures extensively and has participated in field studies across North and Latin America. In 1970 he established the Reptilian Breeding and Research Institute, a private facility. Since its inception, more than 200 species of reptiles and amphibians have been bred at the RBRI, some for the first time in the United States under captive conditions. Successes at the RBRI include several endangered species. Bartlett is a member of numerous herpetological and conservation organizations, cohost of an online reptile and amphibian forum, and a contributing editor of *Reptiles* magazine.

Patricia Bartlett grew up chasing lizards on vacant lots in New Mexico, an area devoid of monitors and tegus, which she admits "was probably a good thing, or I would have chased them as well." After receiving her bachelor's degree from Colorado State University, she moved to Florida to further explore the field of herpetology. She has authored or coauthored some 45 books, most of which deal with reptiles and amphibians.

Acknowledgments

To Bill Love (Blue Chameleon Ventures), Rob MacInnes and Robbie Keszey (Glades, Herp, Inc.), Brian Maddox (Snakes, Inc.), and Dan Scolaro, we extend thanks for the photographic opportunities. MacInnes, Love, and Chuck Hurt unhesitatingly provided us with information about their breeding programs for Merten's and "Ionides" monitors and red tegus. Bert and Hester Langerwerf of Agama International shared their thoughts on breeding black and white tegus. We are also grateful to longtime "varaniphile" and researcher Robert G. Sprackland, who provided us with discussion and research papers.

Important Notes

Caution should be exercised before using any of the electrical equipment described in this book. While handling monitors and tegus, you may occasionally receive bites or scratches. If your skin is broken, see your physician immediately. Some terrarium plants may be harmful to the skin or mucous membranes of human beings. If you notice any signs or irritation, wash the area thoroughly. See your physician if the condition persists. Monitors and tegus may transmit certain infections to humans. Always wash your hands carefully after handling your specimens. Always supervise children who wish to observe your lizards.

Photo Credits

All interior photos by R. D. Bartlett.

Cover Photos

Front and back, front inside and back inside: Zig Leszczynski.

Additional illustrations supplied by Michele Earle-Bridges and Tom Kerr.

All inquiries should be addressed to:
Barron's Educational Series, Inc.
250 Wireless Boulevard
Hauppauge, NY 11788
www.barronseduc.com

ISBN-13: 978-0-7641-3398-5
ISBN-10: 0-7641-3398-5

Library of Congress Catalog Card No. 2006045735

Library of Congress Cataloging-in-Publication Data
Bartlett, Richard D., 1938–
 Monitors, tegus, and related lizards : everything about selection, care, nutrition, diseases, breeding, and behavior / R.D. & Patricia P. Bartlett; illustrations by Laura Barghusen. — 2nd ed.
  p. cm. (A complete pet owner's manual)
 Includes bibliographical references (p.) and index.
 ISBN-13: 978-0-7641-3398-5
 ISBN-10: 0-7641-3398-5
 1. Monitor lizards as pets. 2. Tegus as pets.
3. Lizards as pets. I. Title. II. Series. III. Series: Bartlett, Patricia Pope, 1949.

SF459.L5B37 2006
639.3'9596—dc22   2006045735

Printed in China
9 8 7 6 5 4 3 2 1